Unmasking the Manosphere

The rise of toxic male influencers and the Manosphere means that all over the country, boys are at risk of misogynistic radicalisation. Schools need to be proactive in their efforts to combat misogyny, and this book will help them do just that. It explains how misogyny shows up in classrooms, corridors, and group chats, and, crucially, what we can do to challenge it.

Combining the latest research, personal anecdote, and expert advice, the book provides guidance on tackling misogyny in all aspects of school life from the curriculum and behaviour policies to the corridors and tutor time. Packed with evidence-based strategies and real examples, the chapters cover:

- The Manosphere: what is it and what can we do about it?
- Social media, internet porn, and the role of influencers
- The impact of misogyny on young people
- Combatting misogyny and sexual harassment
- How to have meaningful and effective discussions

Written by Matt Pinkett, teacher, bestselling author, and expert on adolescent masculinity, this is essential reading for teachers and school leaders wanting to better understand, discuss, and address misogyny and sexual harassment in their schools.

Matt Pinkett is a teacher, author, and speaker specialising in issues of masculinity, education, and student wellbeing. With over a decade of classroom experience, Matt has developed a reputation for tackling some of the most complex challenges facing schools today – ranging from boys' underachievement to toxic masculinity, misogyny, and mental health.

'This book acts as a stark yet necessary insight and tool for all educators. As a young female teacher who has been sexually harassed multiple times, it's refreshing to see a male teacher call for schools and government to do more to protect teachers *and* students whilst encouraging classrooms built on empathy, understanding, and respect. Honest, real-life testimonies and practical tips and scripts make some really heavy issues as easily digestible as they can be whilst not shying away from the terrifying reality of misogyny in our schools.'
Georgia Theodoulou, *Teacher and award-winning VAWG campaigner*

'Timely and compelling, this book tackles the challenge of misogyny with clarity, compassion, and conviction. It offers accessible insights and practical strategies to help boys and schools become active agents of change. While fully acknowledging the seriousness and scale of the issue, it never loses sight of the potential for progress. Grounded in realism but driven by hope, this is an indispensable guide that empowers educators and communities to take meaningful action, making it an invaluable resource for anyone committed to fostering respect, equality, and lasting cultural transformation.'
Lisa Sugiura, *Professor in Cybercrime and Gender*

'A sober reminder of the content accessible within a few clicks for many young people in our settings. Rather than turning a blind eye, wishing it weren't the case, we need insights about the nature of the problem. We also need to understand the vulnerability of many young people drawn to the Manosphere: it's often related loneliness and deep sadness. So, what can schools do? There are no quick fixes, but expert insights and advice grounded in the belief that young people need to be heard, taken seriously, and feel that they belong. Those of us working in schools need to know about the Manosphere and we also need support to navigate it. We have both from Matt Pinkett, one of the deepest thinkers and practitioners on this subject.'
Mary Myatt, *Education writer and speaker*

'This book is such an important read. It challenges outdated ideas of masculinity with honesty and compassion while giving teachers (and parents) the tools they need to help boys embrace empathy and authenticity. As someone passionate about gender equality and raising the next generation, I can't recommend it enough.'

Ashley James, *Broadcaster*

Unmasking the Manosphere

Tackling the Misogyny Crisis in Schools

Matt Pinkett

Routledge
Taylor & Francis Group

LONDON AND NEW YORK

Designed cover image: © Lisa Dynan

First published 2026
by Routledge
4 Park Square, Milton Park, Abingdon, Oxon OX14 4RN

and by Routledge
605 Third Avenue, New York, NY 10158

Routledge is an imprint of the Taylor & Francis Group, an informa business

© 2026 Matt Pinkett

The right of Matt Pinkett to be identified as author of this work has been asserted in accordance with sections 77 and 78 of the Copyright, Designs and Patents Act 1988.

All rights reserved. No part of this book may be reprinted or reproduced or utilised in any form or by any electronic, mechanical, or other means, now known or hereafter invented, including photocopying and recording, or in any information storage or retrieval system, without permission in writing from the publishers.

For Product Safety Concerns and Information please contact our EU representative GPSR@taylorandfrancis.com. Taylor & Francis Verlag GmbH, Kaufingerstraße 24, 80331 München, Germany.

Trademark notice: Product or corporate names may be trademarks or registered trademarks, and are used only for identification and explanation without intent to infringe.

British Library Cataloguing-in-Publication Data
A catalogue record for this book is available from the British Library

ISBN: 978-1-041-00853-8 (hbk)
ISBN: 978-1-041-00847-7 (pbk)
ISBN: 978-1-003-61195-0 (ebk)

DOI: 10.4324/9781003611950

Typeset in Optima
by KnowledgeWorks Global Ltd.

May the Men You Meet Be Better

Contents

	Acknowledgements	x
	Introduction	1
1	The Manosphere	17
2	Alpha Males, Algorithms, and Adult Content: How Influencers and Porn Are Warping Boyhood	51
3	Sexual Harassment in Schools and What to Do About It	75
4	Discussing Misogyny	115
5	Male Violence Against Women and Girls	131
6	The Road Ahead	163
	Index	*168*

Acknowledgements

Thanks to those who have loved me, even when I wasn't worthy of your love.

Introduction

A Woman Called Soma

When my first book, *Boys Don't Try? Rethinking Masculinity in Schools* (*BDT?*), was published back in 2019, it wasn't long before I found myself being invited into schools across the length and breadth of the country to talk to teachers about the topics contained within the book. Whether it be advising teachers on how to engage boys in the classroom, helping teachers to better understand some of the mental health challenges that boys face, or getting teachers to confront their own unconscious biases that position boys as academically deficient, schools were eager to work to fix the issues that *BDT?* highlighted.

There was, however, one issue in the book that schools seemed oddly determined to ignore: in the chapter 'Sex and Sexism', I argued that schools were laying the foundations of rape-culture Britain. Some might view this as controversial, but if it was, it wasn't controversial enough to encourage school leaders to engage with the discussion; not one school invited me in to speak about the catastrophe, as I termed it in *BDT?*, that was sexual harassment in schools. Violence was up for discussion. Suicide and self-harm were something we could interrogate. Schools even seemed receptive to my talks on the way teacher bias can have a severe detrimental impact on many student cohorts. But sexual harassment in schools? No. Not at all. Not a chance.

And then along came a woman called Soma.

On Monday 8 June 2020, the BBC screened the first episode of a television series called *I May Destroy You*. The comedy-drama, which follows a young writer's attempts to rebuild her life after a man rapes her, went on to become a huge success and would later be named the sixth greatest series of the 21st century according to one poll. By all accounts, the show's appeal lay in its unflinching approach to shining a light on a society in which men routinely harass, exploit, and abuse women, without reproach.

Luckily for society, one of the thousands of people who watched *I May Destroy You* was a young woman named Soma Sara. The issues the show highlighted prompted 22-year-old Sara and her female friends to reflect on their own experiences of sexual harassment in rape-culture Britain. Sara began to share stories of her and her friends' experiences of sexual harassment on the social media platform Instagram, in order to raise awareness of the way society normalises the violation of female boundaries. As Sara would say in an interview given just three months after her first Instagram post on the matter:

> The London my friends and I grew up in was characterised by an endemic rape culture. Misogyny and sexism was the bedrock of this culture – an unforgiving, ruthless environment where everyone was complicit in the violence that thrived ... I wanted to do everything in my power to continue this essential conversation by giving these stories a more permanent platform.[1]

This permanent platform became the website *Everyone's Invited*. It didn't take long for Sara to realise that it wasn't only London where rape culture thrived – within one week of sharing her own experiences on Instagram, Sara had received over 300 messages from other

Introduction

victims of sexual harassment detailing their experiences. Realising that women wanted a space to confront and discuss the abuse and assaults inflicted upon them, Sara created *Everyone's Invited*, a website which invited users to submit anonymous testimonies of their own experiences of sexual harassment. These testimonies are published on the website and can be viewed by anyone:

> *He cornered me in the bathroom and forced me to let him look at my private areas. He touched it and felt it. I couldn't do anything about it.*
> 27 October 2024, United Kingdom

> *A boy in my school was sat in the back of a lesson with me and started masturbating 20cm away from me as nobody else was in the back row. I froze and couldn't do anything and my school didn't even give him a punishment or write it on a record.*
> 7 September 2024, United Kingdom

> *I was 13 and a group of boys would thrust their hips when I bent over and call me a slut and whore. I went to the pastoral support worker but they said, 'no one at your age would be doing that.' It hurt me so bad knowing they didn't believe me. The boys did it in front of teachers as well and no one did anything.*
> 1 September 2024, Scotland

> *I was 14 and on the bus home from school. A boy in the year below who was sat down to the side of me stuck his hand up my skirt. There was no communication and I just got off the bus. I wonder if he even remembers this act, but it had a huge impact on me.*
> 20 July 2024, United Kingdom

> *I was pinned against a fence when I was in year 2 by a boy in year 3 as he tried to touch me and forced me to kiss him as I cried and hit him.*
> 19 July 2024, United Kingdom.[2]

Unmasking the Manosphere

Noticing that huge swathes of the incidences of sexual harassment described in the testimonies took place in schools, Sara and the team at *Everyone's Invited* decided to publish an annual list of the schools named in readers' submissions. All of a sudden, schools, media outlets, and official bodies started to pay attention. Schools now had to face up to the fact that, as we'll soon see, sexual harassment in schools is not only normalised and commonplace, but rife.

What initially started as one woman's attempt to take a stand is now a movement. A movement which, since its inception, has received over 50,000 written testimonies from victims of sexual harassment; a movement which has prompted British school inspectorate Ofsted to conduct a review of sexual harassment in schools; a movement which, at last count, shone a light on the scourge of sexual harassment taking place in roughly 6,000 British schools.

WHAT IS A RAPE CULTURE?

The charity Rape Crisis England and Wales (RCEW) define a rape culture as:

> ...a culture where sexual violence and abuse is normalised and played down. Where it is accepted, excused, laughed off or not challenged enough by society as a whole.[3]

While the emphasis on acts of sexual violence and sexual abuse, such as rape or sexual touching without consent, is crucial in highlighting the harmful impacts of a rape culture, the definition does ignore other facets of a rape culture which we need to be equally aware of. Here is a list of other signs that you might be living within a rape-culture society:

- Victim blaming ('She shouldn't have worn a short skirt if she wasn't up for it!')

Introduction

- Sexual assault is trivialised ('Boys will be boys!')
- People tell sexually explicit jokes, publicly, and without ensuring consent
- False rape report statistics are inflated
- Victims of rape or sexual assault are scrutinised unfairly
- Masculinity is defined as dominant and sexually aggressive
- Femininity is defined as submissive and sexually passive
- Men are pressured to be sexually promiscuous and experienced
- It is assumed that only promiscuous women are raped
- It is assumed that men don't get raped or that only weak men get raped
- Rape accusations aren't taken seriously
- Women are taught to avoid rape (as opposed to men being taught not to rape)[4]

RCEW draw attention to the fact that in England and Wales, 1 in 4 women has been raped or sexually assaulted (the figure for men is 1 in 18), and that 1 in 6 children have been sexually abused. They also point out that '9 in 10 girls and young women in schools say sexist name-calling and being sent unwanted "dick pics" and other images of a sexual nature happens to them or other girls their age'. According to RCEW, the fact that 'just 1 in 100 rapes recorded by the police result in a charge – let alone a conviction' is evidence that 'rape is essentially decriminalised in England and Wales'.

Ofsted

In their *Review of Sexual Abuse in Schools and Colleges*,[5] published in June 2021, one year after Soma Sara first watched *I May Destroy You*, British school inspectorate Ofsted visited 32 schools and spoke to over 900 pupils, as well as teachers, school leaders, and governors, in an attempt to better understand the extent of the problem of sexual violence, sexual harassment, and sexual abuse in Britain's schools.

To me, and no doubt to many other teachers working in schools, the results of the review were unsurprising. Sexual harassment and online sexual abuse were deemed to be 'prevalent' enough 'that for some children, incidents are so commonplace that they see no point in reporting them'. Ninety per cent of the girls Ofsted spoke to said that 'being sent explicit pictures or videos of things they did not want to see happens a lot or sometimes to them or their peers'. For boys this figure was nearly 50%. Sexual abuse wasn't limited to phone interchanges: '92% of girls said sexist name-calling happens a lot or sometimes to them or their peers.'

Girls in the study reported that most sexual violence they encountered occurred in spaces outside of school, such as parks or at parties, but also that unwanted touching of a sexual nature does occur within school corridors. The review found that most girls don't want to report sexual abuse, violence, or harassment, even when schools encourage them to do so. This is mostly for fear of bullying and social ostracism, but also because they believe that they won't be treated fairly or impartially by the adults in the school.

What's interesting as much as it is concerning is the dissonance the review discovered between teachers' and pupils' perception of the problem of sexual harassment. The review acknowledged that some of the teachers and school leaders they spoke to 'underestimated' the scale of the problem that sexual harassment posed in their setting. Teachers' inability to properly grasp the extent to which sexual harassment occurs in their schools is in marked contrast to how ubiquitous girls realise it is. Girls' responses to survey questions about how often sexual harassment occurs paints a disturbing picture, one that teachers should spend some time scrutinising. In the review, girls were asked whether the following types of harmful

Introduction

sexual behaviour happened 'a lot' or 'sometimes' between people their age. Here's what they said:

Non-contact forms [of harmful sexual behaviour], but face-to-face:
- Sexist name-calling (92%)
- Rumours about their sexual activity (81%)
- Unwanted or inappropriate comments of a sexual nature (80%)

Non-contact forms [of harmful sexual behaviour], online or on social media:
- Being sent pictures or videos they did not want to see (88%)
- Being put under pressure to provide sexual images of themselves (80%)
- Having pictures or videos that they sent being shared more widely without their knowledge or consent (73%)
- Being photographed or videoed without their knowledge or consent (59%)
- Having pictures or videos of themselves that they did not know about being circulated (51%)

Contact forms [of harmful sexual behaviour]:
- Sexual assault of any kind (79%)
- Feeling pressured to do sexual things that they did not want to (68%)
- Unwanted touching (64%)

SEXUAL VIOLENCE, SEXUAL ASSAULT, AND SEXUAL HARASSMENT

Sexual Violence: An umbrella term used to describe any sexual activity that happens without consent. This does not have to be physical. It includes:

- Child sexual abuse
- Rape

> - Sexual assault (see below)
> - Sexual harassment (see below)
> - Female Genital Mutilation (FGM)
> - Sexual Exploitation
> - Sex Trafficking
> - Indecent exposure or 'flashing'
>
> **Sexual Assault:** Sexual assault happens when someone either touches another person in a sexual manner without consent or makes another person touch them in a sexual manner without consent. It includes unwanted kissing and the touching of someone's genitals, breast, or bottom. A type of sexual violence.
>
> **Sexual Harassment:** Any unwanted sexual behaviour that makes someone feel upset, scared, offended, or humiliated, or is meant to make them feel that way. A type of sexual violence.
>
> Source: Rape Crisis England and Wales[6]

The review did also ask boys the same questions about the frequency of these things occurring and noted that boys were 'much less likely' to view these things as happening often. For example, while 79% of girls thought that sexual assault was something that happened, 'a lot' or 'sometimes', only 38% of boys thought the same. Similarly, while 64% of girls felt that unwanted physical touching was something that happened 'a lot' or 'often', this was true for only 24% of boys. This seems to imply that predominantly, it is girls who are the victims of sexual harassment in schools. This implication is correct. While of course boys can be victims of sexual harassment, in *Keeping Children Safe in Education*,[7] published by the Department for Education (DfE), the government does draw

Introduction

attention to the fact that, 'it is more likely girls will be the victims of sexual violence and sexual harassment and more likely it will be perpetrated by boys'.

UK Feminista

In 2017, some three or four years before *Everyone's Invited* and Ofsted raised awareness of the sexual harassment in schools, and two years before I wrote, in *BDT?*, of a 'toxic rape culture that can linger, like a noxious mist, over the classrooms and playgrounds of our schools[8]', UK Feminista, an organisation dedicated to eradicating sexual harassment from schools, had already published their seminal report on the topic of sexual harassment, *'It's Just Everywhere'*.[9]

The report, published in conjunction with the National Education Union (NEU), is a 32-page slap in the face for anybody blind to the rampant sexual harassment in schools. Some frightening statistics stand out:

- Over a third (37%) of female students at mixed-sex schools have personally experienced some form of sexual harassment at school.
- Almost a quarter (24%) of female students at mixed-sex schools have been subjected to unwanted physical touching of a sexual nature while at school.

Perhaps more frightening is the fact that, of the girls in the study who had experienced sexual harassment, only 14% had ever told a teacher. That is to say, 86% of **children** who have been sexually harassed in British schools have just kept schtum. They've been harassed and assaulted and then, filled with shame, rage, and humiliation, just carried on and got on with it. That's what happens in a rape culture.

Unmasking the Manosphere

Girls' reluctance to report what's happened to them is understandable given the report's worrying findings into teachers and sexual harassment:

- Over half (64%) of secondary school teachers are unsure or unaware of the existence of any policies and practices in their school related to preventing sexism.
- Just one in five (20%) secondary school teachers has received training in recognising and tackling sexism as part of their Initial Teacher Education.

In my experience, and as we'll discuss in more depth later in this book, one of the reasons 64% of teachers are unaware of any policies in relation to preventing sexism is probably because they simply don't exist. Behaviour policies, racism policies, and homophobia policies can be found on most school websites. Policies relating to the prevention of sexual harassment and sexism, however, are hard to find.

When secondary school teachers were asked about the barriers to tackling sexism, they cited, among other things, workload being too high to tackle it (yes, really) and the failure of school leadership to make tackling sexism a priority.

It should be pointed out that the problem of sexual harassment in schools isn't limited to child-on-child abuse incidents. A report published jointly by Unison and UK Feminista in 2024 found that one in ten support workers in schools had been sexually harassed at work, mainly by male pupils.[10] We'll look in more depth at child-on-adult sexual harassment in Chapter 3.

Male Violence Against Women and Girls

Sexual harassment isn't the only way girls and women suffer at the hands of men and boys.

Introduction

In July 2024, the National Police Chief's Council (NPCC) released a report in which they declared that Violence Against Women and Girls (VAWG) has reached 'epidemic levels in England and Wales, in terms of its scale, complexity and impact on victims'.[11] They drew attention to a 37% increase in VAWG-related crimes between 2018/19 and 2022/23. The report stated that 1 in every 12 women will be a victim of VAWG per year, but the exact number will likely be higher. While the report listed rape and sexual offences as one of the biggest threats faced by women, it also mentions domestic abuse, stalking and harassment, child sexual abuse and exploitation, and online and tech-enabled VAWG.

What Needs to Change

The truth is that too many schools still treat misogyny as a girls' issue. We write safeguarding policies about how girls should dress, walk home, or behave on social media, and then we're surprised when boys don't see the problem as theirs. That has to change.

We need to stop thinking that a Respect poster and a one-off workshop will cut it. Misogyny is not an RSE problem; it's a culture problem. That means it requires a whole-school approach: from curriculum to corridors, from tutor time to behaviour policies. It means being brave enough to name things clearly. If a student shares revenge porn, that's not just 'poor decision-making' – that's a form of abuse. If a teacher makes a joke about a girl being 'high maintenance', that's not just banter – it's modelling gendered contempt.

We also need to stop excusing harmful behaviour as 'boys being boys' or blaming girls for 'provoking' attention. We need leadership teams to treat misogyny with the same urgency and clarity that we apply to racism or homophobia. We need to train staff, support victims, engage boys, and use our curriculum to open up conversations that shift thinking over time.

Misogynists Can Change

Misogyny, defined as a contempt or prejudice against women, is the root cause of all the ways women and girls are harmed by men and boys. A lack of respect or, indeed, a complete disregard, for female boundaries is the reason men and boys inflict violence and sexual violence on women and girls. And it's time the education system did something about it. It's time we eradicated misogyny from our classrooms, corridors, and playgrounds.

An alcoholic once told me that he doesn't subscribe to the belief that an alcoholic is always defined as an alcoholic, even after years and years of sobriety: 'If I'm always going to be labelled an alcoholic, why would I ever try to get sober?' I see misogyny this way too. While I believe that those who do wrong should take responsibility for the things they have done, I don't believe that misogynistic boys and men need always be misogynistic boys and men. Conversely, I believe that in the same way it can help alcoholics to become sober, a complex interweaving of hard work, support, education, and deep, deep levels of introspection can help boys and men to triumph against the misogyny that may have previously been a quite integral part of their character, how they approached life, and how they interacted with – and mistreated – women.

My commitment to this belief isn't entirely unselfish: every day, I reflect upon the ways I have treated females in the past and I sincerely believe that the shame and guilt I feel about my own misogynistic behaviour will never leave me. I tell you this not in order to glean sympathy or atonement, but so that you, the reader, can see me as living testament to the fact that boys and men can make efforts to change.

What This Book Offers – And Why It Matters

This book doesn't just name the problem of misogyny in schools. It shows teachers what to do about it. It offers teachers a clear, research-informed guide to understanding how misogyny shows up

Introduction

in classrooms, corridors, and group chats and, crucially, how we can challenge it. It's designed for busy teachers, not academics. That means practical strategies, real examples, and language that respects the intelligence and emotional labour of people who work in schools every day.

This isn't a book that demands perfection. It's a book that invites courage and offers concrete steps towards building a school culture where misogyny is challenged early, safely, and persistently.

Chapter Outlines

In Chapter 1, we'll look at the **Manosphere** – a dark and murky area of the internet ostensibly dedicated to the improvement of male lives, but which has become something far darker. Here, we'll learn about groups of men and boys whose ideologies are as bewildering as the acronyms used to describe them: PUAs, MGTOWs, MRAs, and Incels. In getting to understand these groups and what they believe, we'll be better placed to help boys at risk of radicalisation from these groups.

After that, in Chapter 2 we'll explore the problem of **toxic male influencers** but also the impact of social media and internet porn on facilitating misogynistic attitudes.

Chapter 3 will delve deep into the issue of **misogyny in schools**. We'll explore what it looks like, what schools are doing to perpetuate it, and how we can combat it. As with my previous books, the solutions offered will be practical and written not only for school leaders and pastoral staff but also for teachers working at the chalk face. It is my belief that whole-school cultural shift can only occur when we think about those not in positions where change can be directly enacted. *What can Miss Ahmed in Maths do to change the way boys in her Year 8 class talk to the girls in the class? What can Ms Jones do, as they're on playground duty, to ensure that the boys and girls in Year 11 are relating to each other*

Unmasking the Manosphere

consensually and respectfully? What can Mr Ashworth, in History, do when a girl approaches him at the end of the lesson to tell him that another girl called her a slut?

In Chapter 4, we'll learn how to have **effective discussions about misogyny**. Teachers come from a diverse range of gender, cultural, and religious backgrounds as well as having differing experiences of sexual experience and sexual abuse. It can often be difficult to know what to say or what not to say, and this chapter aims to make anybody who reads it feel more comfortable about discussing topics such as misogyny, consent, and HSB with students.

In Chapter 5, we'll explore the issue of **male violence against women and girls** and how schools can ensure that the scourge of male-on-female violence becomes a thing of the past.

Finally, in Chapter 6, we'll look to **the road ahead** and what we can all do, going forward, to ensure we remain consistent and determined in our efforts to rid our schools of the scourge of misogyny.

What I Hope You'll Take Away

I want readers to finish this book feeling equipped, not overwhelmed. Too often, teachers are told to tackle enormous social issues without being given the tools to do so. With misogyny, we're often left with vague slogans like 'promote respect' or 'celebrate diversity' and no real clarity on how to intervene when a Year 10 boy calls a girl a 'slut' under his breath mid lesson. This book is about giving you the *how*.

I want you to feel more confident calling things out, more skilled at calling students in, and more hopeful that your actions make a difference. I hope you'll see that tackling misogyny isn't a separate job from the day-to-day work of teaching, but that it's *part of* helping children grow into better humans. I hope this book sparks staffroom conversations, curriculum reviews, and whole-school

Introduction

thinking about the kind of environment we're really building for our students.

If there's one message I want to land, it's this: even small moments matter. You don't need to deliver TED Talks or rewrite your entire PSHE scheme. If you can respond to a sexist joke with calm authority, if you can help a boy understand how porn has shaped his expectations of girls, if you can create a classroom where girls feel seen and boys feel safe to unlearn – then you're already doing the work.

The Difference Schools Can Make

Schools are where gender roles get rehearsed and re-enforced, but they can also be where they get rewritten. Boys don't just learn misogyny from social media. They learn it from each other, in whispered jokes and group chats. But they also watch how adults respond. They notice when we laugh things off, when we ignore the quiet comments, when we fail to step in. They also notice when we get it right.

The impact of challenging misogyny in schools isn't just about individual students. It's about shaping the next generation of men and the girls who grow up alongside them. A school that teaches boys to respect boundaries, take responsibility, and speak out against sexism doesn't just create a safer school: It creates a safer society.

I've spent years visiting schools and talking to boys about masculinity, sex, consent, and power. And if there's one thing I've learned, it's that they are crying out for guidance. Boys are not unreachable. But they are confused, conflicted, and surrounded by digital noise that we can't afford to ignore. If we don't fill the silence with something honest, human, and hopeful, then someone else will fill it with rage.

Unmasking the Manosphere

Teachers can't do everything. But we can do something. And this book exists to help you figure out what your something looks like – in your classroom, in your corridor, in your school.

Because when it comes to misogyny, silence is a lesson too. And it's one we can no longer afford to teach.

Notes

1. www.lastbusmagazine.com/allposts/kgtnp999839p4h3sy8qcqn7i0uk704
2. www.everyonesinvited.uk/submissions/read
3. https://rapecrisis.org.uk/get-informed/about-sexual-violence/what-is-rape-culture/
4. https://inside.southernct.edu/sexual-misconduct/facts
5. www.gov.uk/government/publications/review-of-sexual-abuse-in-schools-and-colleges/review-of-sexual-abuse-in-schools-and-colleges
6. https://rapecrisis.org.uk/
7. www.gov.uk/government/publications/keeping-children-safe-in-education--2
8. Pinkett, M., & Roberts, M. (2019) *Boys don't try? Rethinking masculinity in schools.* Routledge, p. 119.
9. https://ukfeminista.org.uk/wp-content/uploads/2017/12/Report-Its-just-everywhere.pdf
10. www.unison.org.uk/content/uploads/2024/06/Sexisminschoolssurveyreport1.pdf
11. National Police Chief's Council. (2024). *National Policing Statement 2024 for Violence Against Women and Girls (VAWG).*

1 The Manosphere

8 Ways to Be an Alpha Male.
7 Proven Tips to Attract Any Girl.
The 23 Habits of a Stylish Man.
Ultimate Guide to Father's Rights in the UK.
How Can a Teenage Guy Become More Attractive?

The internet abounds with articles, videos, discussion forums, and blog and social media posts dedicated to improving men's lives. Helping men navigate the tricky areas of relationships, fashion, physical attractiveness, divorce proceedings, and custody battles, collectively, these web pages make up what is informally known as the 'Manosphere'.

Despite sounding like the name of a zany 90's Saturday night TV show, in actual fact there are sections of the Manosphere that are anything but what a reasonable person might consider fun. Sections of the Manosphere are filled with anti-female discourse and misogynistic rhetoric spewed by people – mostly men – each of whom belongs to any one of a number of toxic Manosphere communities, each with their own language and belief systems.

What began as a positive online space is now, as Lisa Sugiura explains in her book *The Incel Rebellion: The Rise of the*

Unmasking the Manosphere

Manosphere and the Virtual War Against Women, 'a decentralised network of websites, gaming platforms and chat rooms imbued with misogyny and satire, and a compelling overlap with other violent ideologies'.[1] Now, the Manosphere is a place where men give each other advice on how to rape women; a place where men decry domestic violence statistics as either inflated or downright false; a place where men use pseudo-scientific evidence to explain female inferiority; a place where men blurt out bizarre conspiracy theories about female-centric plots to destroy masculinity in all its forms.

Worryingly, much of the most disturbing Manosphere content is easily accessible. It took me just one Google search, two clicks of a mouse, and a little under 30 seconds to access discussion forums with the following titles, without any sort of age verification check, password, or sign-up required:

- *Women did this to us. With revenge in mind women reduced us to the level of insects. They WILL pay for what they've done with punishments worse than death.*
- *Mothers Abuse & Kill Children – Mainly Males – More.*
- *Women gain sexual pleasure from the pain that is inflicted upon them.*
- *Females are Psychopaths – A Socio-Historic Review.*
- *[STUDY] Women convince other women to look like ugly dykes to wipe out intersexual competition (and how they artificially inflate the price of sex).*

It might be reasonable, or comforting, to think that the people engaging with Manosphere content like this are nothing more than a small group of sad, lonely weirdos whose influence is limited only to the online space they occupy. Sadly, however, to think like this would be to underestimate the very real threat that the Manosphere and its communities presents to the boys we teach, the boys we raise, and the men they will one day become.

Prevent and the Manosphere

Prevent is a national initiative, created by the UK government, which aims to stop young people from being drawn into extremism and terrorism. When a school feels that their own in-house interventions are not sufficient to protect a child at risk of radicalisation, or who has already been radicalised, they are duty bound to make what's known as a Prevent referral. Once a referral has been made to Prevent, a team of social workers, school leaders, and police officers known as the Channel Panel will then decide if the referral is serious enough to be taken on as a case. If this decision is made, then the Channel Panel will convene to decide and facilitate the best course of action to help intervene and protect the child at risk.

To fully comprehend the threat that the Manosphere poses to young people, we can look at recent Prevent statistics around 'incel-related concerns'. The term 'incel' is a portmanteau of the words 'involuntary' and 'celibate', and as we'll soon discover, men who identify as incels are members of a (predominantly) online community of men who believe they are unable to attract women sexually and romantically because they are genetically lacking in the areas women find attractive. This belief, in turn, breeds much bitterness and resentment, and as a result, incels are extremely hostile towards women. On incel chatrooms, men will talk openly about their hatred for women and their desire to inflict violence, death, or rape upon them.

The latest available Prevent statistics,[2] published by the government in December 2024 for the period April 2023 to March 2024, showed that of the 6,922 referrals made to Prevent in that time frame, only 54 (1%) were for incel-related concerns. This small proportion may inspire little concern. However, even though incel-related concerns accounted for the smallest number of Prevent referrals, incel-related referrals are the most likely type of concern to be taken on as serious cases by the Channel Panel, with 64% of incel referrals being adopted as a case.

Unmasking the Manosphere

In order to better respond to the threat that incels present to young people, we need to better understand the Manosphere, but before we examine Manosphere groups in more detail, we first need to be absolutely clear on a few central beliefs, upon which nearly all Manosphere ideologies are founded. First up, it's time to look into the metaphorical, misogynistic, and downright mad world of the Manosphere medicine cabinet...

Blue and Red Pills

The Wachowski sisters' blockbuster 1999 movie *The Matrix* is set in a dystopian future where, nearly a century earlier, powerful robots enslaved humanity. To harvest humans' bioelectric energy without resistance, the invading machines created 'The Matrix' – a simulated reality fed directly into people's minds, convincing them they're living normal lives while, in fact, their bodies are imprisoned in pods where they are drained of their lifeforce. The story follows Neo, played by Keanu Reeves, a computer hacker who encounters Morpheus, a rebel leader intent on freeing mankind from robot dominion. Morpheus offers Neo a choice: take the blue pill to forget their meeting and continue living in the illusion or take the red pill to awaken to the harsh truth – that the world he knows is a simulation designed to conceal humanity's enslavement by machines.

In a striking irony, the misogynistic, often transphobic individuals within Manosphere communities have co-opted the concept of red and blue pills, originally created by the trans female Wachowski sisters, as a central pillar of their worldview.

In the Manosphere, men who have swallowed the metaphorical blue pill are seen as wilfully blind to a supposed fundamental truth: that we live in a female-centric society where men are devalued to the point of disposability. In this worldview, power lies with manipulative and superficial women who use it to humiliate, deceive, and exploit men. Only those who have taken the metaphorical red pill are believed to have 'woken up' and are therefore able to see this hidden reality for what it is. For men who have swallowed the red pill, every social interaction is reframed as part of a rigged game. It positions women as predators and men as victims, telling those who take it that bitterness and resentment towards women is not only justified but enlightened.

It's important to note that the red pill isn't just doom and resentment – it also sells a way out. The message is simple: if you accept the 'truth' that the world is unfairly stacked in women's favour, you can hack the system. Lift weights, make money, develop ruthless confidence and, they promise, you'll stop being invisible. In other words, it's a self-improvement project, but one built on bitterness: become desirable, not for connection or kindness, but to 'win' at a game you believe is rigged against you.

The Black Pill

While most Manosphere communities adhere to red-pill ideologies, one Manosphere group swallow a different medicine. Dissatisfied with what they see as the red pill's false hope, incels have concocted a more nihilistic alternative: the *black* pill. For incels, the black pill represents a worldview where not only are the harsh realities of male disadvantage exposed, but they are also deemed permanent and unchangeable. In the eyes of black-pill swallowers, no amount of self-improvement, social awareness, or development of 'game' – the ability to seduce women – can overcome the brutal force of genetic and societal bias. For many incels, they are irrevocably doomed to a life of romantic failure.

Hypergamy and the 80:20 Principle

A central belief of red and black-pill ideology is the concept of hypergamy – the idea that women are evolutionarily programmed to seek sexual or romantic partners with a higher Sexual Market

Unmasking the Manosphere

Value (SMV) than their own. Red-pillers have simplified this into what they call the 80:20 Principle, which claims that 80% of women are only attracted to the top 20% of men – those deemed to have the highest SMV. As a result, they argue, 80% of men are effectively excluded from romantic or sexual relationships. This belief feeds into the narrative that women, due to their supposed greater 'sexual power', can be highly selective, a notion that fuels much of the resentment and bitterness within Manosphere communities.

However, the 80:20 Principle is fundamentally flawed. It originates from economics, where it's known as the Pareto Principle, which states that roughly 80% of outcomes come from 20% of causes. Its misapplication to dating can be traced back to a 2015 blog post titled *Tinder Experiments II: Guys, Unless You Are Really Hot, You're Probably Better Off Not Wasting Your Time on Tinder*,[3] written by an anonymous blogger known as 'Worst-Online-Dater'. In his informal experiment, he created a fake profile on dating app Tinder using photos of a conventionally attractive 26-year-old man. By swiping right on every profile, he secured matches with 22.6% of the women he encountered. He then asked 27 of these matches how many male profiles they typically liked, with the women estimating that they liked around 14% of the profiles they viewed. Based on this small, self-reported dataset (and some questionable economic extrapolations), he concluded that 'the bottom 80% of men are competing for the bottom 22% of women, and the top 78% of women are competing for the top 20% of men'.

In other words, one of the Manosphere's most defining beliefs is built on an unethical, non-scientific experiment with a tiny sample size, biased methodology, and unverifiable self-reported data. Unsurprisingly, given its shaky origins, the 80:20 Principle has been debunked multiple times. A 2019 study by Oxford University,[4] which analysed the dating profiles of 150,000 eHarmony users, found that

The Manosphere

average-looking men were more likely to receive messages than their more conventionally attractive counterparts. Another study of OKCupid data found that although women *are* choosy, they still message men they rate as average.[5] Even on the free-for-all that is Tinder, while the top profiles get the most swipes, researchers found patterns of reciprocity: people mostly aim just slightly above their 'league'.[6] It would be fair to say that although dating is skewed, it's certainly not broken, and certainly not the brutal hierarchy the Manosphere would have us believe it is.

Now, you know about some of the Manosphere's key philosophies and ideas, it's time to take a look at the communities that exist within the space, and the threat they pose to society and young people.

Incels

In the mid-1990s, a Canadian woman, now known only as Alana, created a website called *Alana's Involuntary Celibacy Project*. It was designed as a support space for people who struggled to form intimate and romantic relationships to share dating tips, offer advice, and cope with the challenges of unwanted singlehood. Alana coined the term 'invcel' – a portmanteau of 'involuntary celibate' – to describe the community. The site was a friendly, inclusive environment where both men and women supported one another through feelings of loneliness and isolation.

Eventually, it was agreed that the term 'invcel' was a bit clunky, and so the term 'incel' was born. In its infancy, the term, as Alana later explained in an interview with the BBC, 'used to mean anybody of any gender who was lonely, had never had sex, or who hadn't had a relationship in a long time'.[7] Over the years, the term 'incel' has undergone a drastic transformation. What once served as a friendly label for people struggling with loneliness and dating became appropriated by angry men who, frustrated by their perceived inability to attract women, now use it as a badge of bitter resentment.

Chads, Stacies, and Beckies

Incels boil down dating into a sort of scorecard, where women are ascribed a 'Sexual Market Value', or SMV. In plain terms, it's a rating system – usually on a scale of 1 to 10 – where 10 represents the pinnacle of attractiveness. Women known as '10s' are labelled 'Stacies'. A 'Stacy' is a woman only satisfied with partners with a level of attractiveness way out of reach for the average bloke. Meanwhile, women who incels perceive to be only moderately attractive – somewhere around 5–7 on the SMV scale – are known as 'Beckies'.

Incels also believe that men have their own SMV. According to members of the incel community, while their own SMV is lower than that of most other men, there are a group of men who exist at the apex of the male sexual attractiveness scale. These men are known as 'Chads'. Chads' effortless ability to attract women means that incels resent them almost as deeply as they resent 'Stacies'. Below Chads in their pecking order are the 'Normies', men who, in incel terms, score somewhere between a 4 and a 7 on the physical attractiveness scale. Anyone scoring less than a 4 is essentially an incel, although the numbers vary depending on who you're engaging with or what incel website you're on.

Interestingly, while physical attractiveness is a major factor in a man's SMV, incels also point to wealth, status, and what they call 'game' (or seduction skills) as important components in attracting women. However, unlike Pick-Up Artists (see below) who lean heavily on tricks and strategies to seduce (sorry – manipulate and exploit) women, incels insist that without that key physical appeal, no amount of charm or success will win female attention.

THE HIERARCHY OF MALE ATTRACTIVENESS

It's not just women who find themselves labelled and judged by incels on the basis of perceived attractiveness; men, too, are slotted into a rigid masculine hierarchy, each position defined by its distance from the ideals of dominance and desirability. The hierarchy, as incels see it, is as follows, in ascending order:

Omega Males

Omega males sit at the very bottom of the masculine hierarchy. They carry an awareness of their own inadequacy, revealed through low self-esteem, social awkwardness, and persistent failure in romantic and sexual relationships. Omegas are outsiders, trapped on the margins, and many incels refer to themselves as Omegas – a label that becomes both an identity and a prison. Their isolation breeds resentment, and their frustration curdles into bitterness.

Beta Males

Beta males are the so-called 'average' men: neither repulsive nor remarkable. Less attractive and socially dominant than alphas, they're marked by hesitation, lack of confidence, and struggle in romantic pursuits. In incel spaces, betas are pitied at best and mocked at worst – men who submit rather than lead, doomed to forever play supporting roles in a game rigged in favour of the bold.

Alpha Males

Alpha males are the top of the traditional ladder of attractiveness: dominant, socially magnetic, physically attractive, and effortlessly assertive. Alphas seem to glide through life with women drawn to them and men deferential around them. For many incels, the alpha is both an object of hatred and aspiration – someone to resent for his effortless success, yet someone they long to become.

Sigma Males

If the alpha is the leader of the pack, the sigma is the wolf who walks alone. Sigma males reject the hierarchy entirely, thriving outside of social structures. They are seen as enigmatic, powerful, and self-sufficient, carrying an effortless cool they have no need to prove. Sigmas are the fantasy of untouchable masculinity: handsome, ruthless, and mysterious. Unsurprisingly, incel forums are littered with adoration for fictional sigmas like *American Psycho*'s Patrick Bateman – a wealthy, narcissistic sociopath who tortures women – and *Peaky Blinders'* Tommy Shelby, a brooding, violent gang leader who answers to no one.

Cucks

Cuck is a word that sits outside the formal hierarchy altogether. It's not a position but an insult: the ultimate dismissal of a man perceived as weak, submissive, or lacking masculine authority. In incel spaces, to call someone a cuck is to brand them as contemptible – a man so far removed from power and respect that he becomes an object of ridicule. The term originates from *cuckold*, traditionally referring to a man whose partner is unfaithful. But in these communities, it's spat out as a slur for any man who fails to dominate. It's worth noting that in the kink world, *cuck* refers to a consensual sexual dynamic – but in incel spaces, there is no nuance, only scorn.

Why Do People Become Incels?

Understanding why some young men gravitate towards incel spaces is vital if we want to prevent bitterness from hardening into hatred. Although the term 'incel' conjures images of angry young men, online echo chambers, and violence, these simplistic caricatures miss something more troubling: that often incels are lost and lonely boys or men. Becoming an incel isn't always an ideological choice but the endpoint of years of culminating psychological collapse, social isolation, and cultural grooming. What follows is an explanation of some of the key reasons individuals might gravitate towards inceldom:

1. Chronic Social Rejection and Low Self-Worth

At the root of almost every incel's story is rejection: persistent, humiliating, formative rejection. According to Kalish and Kimmel's study, 'Suicide by mass murder: Masculinity, aggrieved entitlement, and rampage school shootings',[8] this can lead to a phenomenon known as 'aggrieved entitlement' – the belief that one has unjustly been denied affection and intimacy. The rejection isn't merely romantic but social also: many incels have felt on the periphery for most of their lives. They are not just unlucky in love; they are marginalised and humiliated by others because of their bad luck.

2. Poor Mental Health

Many incels are unwell. The empirical data is sobering. One study found that 91% of incels self-reported symptoms of depression, 85% for anxiety and 40% for PTSD.[9]

In Joe Whittaker's interviews (see, *Incels: Who Are They?* below) with 561 incels from the UK and US, he found that over a third of the sample (39%) met the criteria for moderate depression, with 43% having anxiety, based on NHS screening tests. One in five incels in the study had contemplated suicide every day for the past two weeks.[10]

Incels aren't always embittered and angry; many of them are drowning in a world of sadness and nobody's throwing them the buoyancy aids they need to keep them afloat. For others, their world is viewed through a lens coloured by paranoia, worthlessness, and fear. Identifying as an incel brings coherence to the negative feelings that blight their narrative: a script that explains personal suffering in grand, societal terms.

3. Isolation and the Absence of Real-World Social Networks

Incels aren't just rejected by women; they are estranged from everyone. Many incels rely heavily on the online world of the Manosphere for connection instead of leaning on people 'in real life' for support. While these spaces provide the illusion of security and community, they often serve to further sever the connections between incels and the real world.

4. Grooming and Conditioning

Incels don't tend to be formally recruited into the community. Instead, they are groomed by content: 'amusing' memes, pseudo-scientific rants and infographics, and celebratory violence all play a part in turning hopelessness into ideology. Incel forums amplify anger, normalise misogyny, and encourage nihilistic fatalism.[11]

In my own forays into incel forums and social media spaces, I've noted the way any attempts at personal improvement are mocked. Instead, bitterness, resentment, and the simple act of giving up all hopes of self-improvement are revered and elevated as a sign of wisdom. The black pill – the belief that nothing can or should change – becomes gospel in incel spaces.

5. The Allure of Explanation

The incel worldview is seductively simple for men and boys who otherwise feel lonely, confused, and floundering. It essentially tells them: 'Your misery, your loneliness, your failure, is not your fault.' Suddenly, a coherent, if bleak, narrative tidies everything up.

6. Vicarious Validation Through Violence

Finally – and most dangerously – incel spaces offer incels vicarious validation through violent spectacle. Mass murderers are mythologised and become symbolic representations of what every incel secretly or overtly wishes: to be seen, to be feared, to be avenged.

While there are many factors influencing people's decision to identify as incel, very few members of the community want to commit acts of mass violence or murder. In Whittaker's in-depth study of 561 incels, he found that just 5% of incels said that they 'often' justify violence against people they perceive to be causing them harm. The average response sat between 'Never' and 'Rarely'.

However, that's not to say that incels are incapable of violence. Sadly, there have been high-profile cases of incel mass murder and violence, and when such events occur, they are devastating.

Incels and Violence

On 23 May 2014, Elliot Rodger, aged 22, repeatedly stabbed his three flatmates to death. Their names were Cheng Yuan Hong, 20, Weihan Wang, 20, and George Chen, 19. Just after 9 pm on the evening of the same day, Rodger drove to a University of California sorority house with the intention of killing those inside. When he knocked on the door and nobody answered, he started shooting at nearby females, two of whom he killed. Their names were Katherine Cooper and Veronika Weiss and they were just 22 and 19 years of age, respectively. Rodger then got back into his car and drove to a nearby delicatessen, where he shot University of

Unmasking the Manosphere

California student Christopher Michael-Martinez, aged 20. After this, he drove through the town of Isla Vista, shooting at people through the driver's window as he did so. By the time the sheriff's department had shot Rodger dead, he had killed a total of six people and injured fourteen.

In between killing his flatmates and driving to the sorority house, Rodger took the time to email his 107,000-word manifesto, 'My Twisted World: The Story of Elliot Rodger', to a small group of people he knew, including his parents and therapists. The manifesto, as Rodger himself explains, 'is a dark story of sadness, anger, and hatred', in which Rodger attempts to explain the massacre he knew he would soon carry out. Rodger's introduction provides chilling insight into the theme of the text it precedes:

> All of my suffering on this world has been at the hands of humanity, particularly women. It has made me realise just how brutal and twisted humanity is as a species. All I ever wanted was to fit in and live a happy life amongst humanity, but I was cast out and rejected, forced to endure an existence of loneliness and insignificance, all because the females of the human species were incapable of seeing the value in me.

After emailing his manifesto, Rodger then uploaded a video – titled 'Elliot Rodger's Retribution' – to YouTube, in which he outlined his motives for the massacre he was going to commit the following day. The words he speaks are as frightening as those he writes:

> This is my last video. It all has to come to this. Tomorrow is the day of retribution ... ever since I hit puberty I've been forced to endure an existence of loneliness, rejection and unfulfilled desires all because girls have never been attracted to me. Girls gave their affection and sex and love to other men but never to me. I'm 22 years old and I'm still a virgin ... I don't know why you girls aren't attracted to me but I will punish you all for it... you throw yourselves at all these obnoxious men instead of me,

the supreme gentleman ... I will slaughter every single spoiled, stuck-up, blonde slut I see ...

As I watch Rodger's 'last video', I am struck by nature's sick joke: as he calmly and chillingly articulates his desire for 'annihilation', his face is bathed in a soft, golden light filtering through the window of the car that he would, just a few hours later, turn into a weapon. This perverse halo foreshadows the sainthood Rodger now holds in incel circles. On incel forums, he is revered. His initials, *ER*, appear in usernames and thread titles. There are whole posts dedicated to the man incels affectionately term 'the supreme gentleman'. Such is the reverence incels hold for Rodger that his name has even become a verb: to 'go *ER*' is to turn violent fantasy into mass murder.

In the aftermath of his death, it was found that Rodger frequently visited incel forums in which he regularly posted about his resentment for women and his desire to inflict harm and pain upon them.

Here in the UK, it might be tempting to see mass shootings like these as an American problem, which needn't concern us.

To do so would be dangerously naive.

On 12 August 2021, 22-year-old Jake Davison killed five people in the Keyham area of Plymouth, England in a rampage that lasted between eight and twelve minutes. His first victim was his mother, Maxine Davison. He shot her twice. At approximately 6.08 pm, she was dead.

After he left the house, he saw Lee Martyn and his three-year-old daughter, Sophie, on the street. He shot them both. Witnesses later described how their bodies lay, with one witness explaining how as the pair lay dead, Martyn's lifeless arm lay across the body of his little girl, as if cradling her.[12] Davison then went on to shoot and injure Michelle Parker and her son, Ben Parsonage. After that he shot and killed Stephen Washington, a full-time carer for his disabled wife, before finally shooting dead Kate Shepherd. By this point, he had killed one child, two women, and two men.

At 6.24 pm, as police arrived, he shot himself. Six dead.

Dominic Adamson KC, representing the families of Davison's victims, would say at the inquest that Davison's internet history 'refers to violence, misogynistic views, and indicated an extremely hostile relationship between him and his mother. He had explored on numerous occasions mass killings and referred to people idolised in the incel community for perpetrating mass killings.'[13]

I would not be surprised to learn that any teachers or parents who have read to this point are alarmed. Clearly, a belief in incel ideology can have devastating effects. But to what extent are people like Rodger and Davison truly reflective of the threat that incels pose? Are they representative, or are they simply rare and magnified examples of incel violence?

A 2019 study by Jaki et al., titled 'Online hatred of women on the Incels.me forum',[14] examined the violent language used by incels on a popular incel discussion website, *Incels.me*. The study says that in incel forums, 'messages that proliferate misogyny or incite crime help a user to cement his reputation as an alpha user'. In other words, messages of a violent nature, or messages which incite violence, help incels gain acceptance in their section of the Manosphere. A core principle of incel and black-pill culture is the idea that incels exist on the periphery of society, rejected and marginalised because of their genetic deficiencies. This can explain why many incels resort to the language of violence online: it helps them to belong.

Jaki et al. note that the *Incels.me* forum, at the time of her study, was a largely unmoderated space. Unlike Reddit, which has made concerted attempts to shut down incel discussion forums, on *Incels.me*, despite rules prohibiting bullying, racism, and violent content, these rules are 'enforced only half-heartedly', meaning that *Incels.me* 'is rife with hate speech, filled with discussions about hate crime, and offensive infighting'.

Jaki et al.'s study highlights a range of violent comments that the researchers found on the *Incels.me* forum:

- Disobedient wives should be beaten
- I want them all [women] to die
- I'm driven by hate, any action that can lead to the slightest bit of revenge upon society is worth the effort
- They don't give a shit about us. Nobody does. That's why I have no problem if any of us starts killing as many people as possible. The more young women ... who get slaughtered, the better.

Despite the obvious concern that such comments evoke, Jaki et al. do acknowledge that there are incels who do object to violence. One user, they note, says: 'I don't condone violence. Especially mindless violence against innocent people.' Another user thinks that the attention given to people like Rodger ... could play a role in future incel acts of violence: '[the] media makes these killers into overnight celebrities'.

In a 2021 study,[15] Speckhard et al. surveyed 271 incels to better understand the violent threat the incel community might pose. In this study, just 17 of the survey participants (6%) agreed with the statement that incel groups are 'willing to endorse violence', while 46% of the survey participants 'completely disagreed' with the opinion that incels are violent and dangerous. What this could suggest is that mainstream media portrayals of incels as twisted loners out to inflict violence are nothing more than distorted and unrealistic projections informed by a tiny majority of incels – people like Rodger and Davison – who do commit dreadful, and therefore, attention-catching, acts of extreme violence. An alternative explanation is that 46% of incels in the survey simply refused to accept the very real threat that incels present.

This study asked participants to comment on their own violence. Twenty-six per cent of participants agreed with the statement 'I sometimes entertain thoughts of violence towards others.' Disturbingly, 37 of the respondents (13.6%) said that they would rape if they knew they'd get away with it. The likelihood of a participant expressing a desire to rape if they could get away with it increased when a participant declared higher levels of misogyny. Entertaining thoughts of violence also increased if a participant's self-reported misogyny score was higher.

Crucially for teachers and people working in schools whose job it is to nurture and develop children, the study also noted that the incels in the study did suffer 'psychological symptoms': in Speckhard et al.'s study, 64% said they'd experienced depressive symptoms; 28% said they'd experienced PTSD; 60% reported anxiety symptoms; and 48% declared having experienced suicidal thoughts. It is this, no doubt, that led the research team to declare in the report's abstract that 'the threat of violence from a subset of incels should not be ignored, but promotion of compassionate and understanding psychology may be more broadly beneficial to the community'.

What is clear, and important for us, as parents and teachers of boys, to recognise is that incel spaces in the Manosphere *are* violent spaces. They are spaces where men advocate for rape and violence against women. However, such proclamations, on the whole, are symptomatic of a desperate desire for attention and acceptance in a community where such views earn reward and admiration rather than condemnation. In the few studies that have actually asked incels about violence – those studies we've looked at here – the reality is that many incels do not condone violence.

However, there will be a small minority of people for whom inceldom is more than just empty threats of violent retribution and bluster. For this small – but lethal – minority, a complex and toxic mix of immersion in the incel community, encouragement from other incels, and the attention that the community provides transforms empty threats of violent retribution and bluster into three-year-old girls lying dead on the pavement cradled in the arms of the fathers who died trying to protect them.

Incels and Racism

Many incels adopt a victim mentality, convinced that society favours certain groups over others. While this belief most often manifests in the idea that women hold all the power, it also reveals itself in the way incels construct rigid racial hierarchies among themselves.

Within incel communities, there is a common belief that to be attractive to women, you must be white. This leads to both overt racism and the disturbing phenomenon of minority incels expressing extreme self-loathing, openly attributing their lack of romantic success to their race.

Terms like *currycel* (used to demean South Asian men) and *ricecel* (used against East and Southeast Asian men) are common in incel spaces. They reflect a hierarchy in which white men are placed at the top, black men are often portrayed as hypersexualised rivals, and Asian men are relegated to the bottom – dismissed as undesirable by default.

The racism within incel culture highlights a dangerous cycle: internal self-loathing reinforces external hatred, and these communities become echo chambers where bigotry is not only tolerated but celebrated.

INCELS: WHO ARE THEY?

It's difficult to know exactly how many incels there are. Incels are often intensely private. For those incels who openly talk about violence, secrecy is necessary to avoid scrutiny from authorities. For others, who believe in vast conspiracies aimed at destroying men, anonymity is a protection strategy. Tracking numbers is made even harder by the fact that many incel websites – where membership could serve as a rough indicator – are regularly shut down or pushed into the dark web to avoid detection. However, Lisa Sugiura estimates there are around 100,000 incels globally.[16]

In May 2024, Joe Whittaker and his team (see above) published the largest study of incels to date, in an attempt to better understand who they really are.

The study, which analysed data from 561 incels in the US and UK, found most incels to be:

- In their mid-20s
- Heterosexual
- Childless
- Middle or lower class
- Educated to secondary level
- Living at home or renting

Some other interesting things stood out:

Height

Many incels blame their lack of success with women on their height. The average height of incels in the study was 5ft 8 – just one inch below the national average of 5ft 9. This suggests that perceptions of height bias are largely exaggerated in their minds.

Politics

Despite the racist and far-right rhetoric common in incel spaces, participants in this study leaned slightly left of centre politically, expressing progressive views on issues like homosexuality and social benefits. This contradiction shows how confused and inconsistent incel ideology can be – borrowing from both extremes, depending on what suits their narrative of victimhood.

Mental Health

The mental health picture was bleak. As has already been mentioned above, according to NHS diagnostic tools, 39% of incels met the criteria for anxiety and 43% for depression. More than one in five (21.6%) reported having suicidal thoughts every single day. Almost half described themselves as intensely lonely.

Enemies

When asked who they saw as their biggest enemies, 'feminists' topped the list. This was followed by 'the political left', 'wider society', and finally, 'women'.

Violence

When asked, 'Is violence justified against people who harm incels?', 5% of participants said 'often', and a quarter said 'sometimes' or 'often'. The average response fell between 'never' and 'rarely', suggesting that while high-profile cases like Elliot Rodger grab headlines, they don't represent the entire incel community. That said, even small percentages matter – radicalisation often begins in minority mindsets before spilling into mainstream danger.

Connecting

Most incels connect with others through anonymous online forums. Interestingly, nearly one in five (18%) had met another incel in person. This challenges the idea that incels exist purely online. These ideologies can, and do, cross into real-world friendships and conversations.

Analysis

We need to be vigilant. The stereotype of incels as simply right-wing weirdos lurking online isn't the full story. Incels are out there – and they might not look, behave, or think as we expect.

More importantly, we need to make sure boys in our schools are happy. Boys need to feel valued, and we need to help them value themselves and others. They need to feel connected – to each other, to adults, and to the school community. Fostering connection is one of the most powerful protective factors we have.

Incels are just one section of the Manosphere ecosystem, which also includes groups like MGTOWs, MRAs, and PUAs, each with their own rules, grievances, and contradictions. Let's find out more about them.

MGTOWs

MGTOW (pronounced 'Mig-Tau'), which stands for 'Men Going Their Own Way', is a philosophy that encourages men to prioritise their own lives and interests over traditional societal expectations, especially those related to relationships with women. Men who are advocates of the MGTOW movement refer to themselves as MGTOWs, and they believe that modern society is structured in a way that is detrimental to men. They argue that marriage, cohabitation, dating, and even platonic and professional relationships with women are simply too risky for men; for MGTOWs it's much easier to reject relationships with women altogether. If incels' inability to form relationships with women is involuntary, for MGTOWs, it's an active choice. MGTOWs' refusal to engage with women isn't just about avoiding relationships; it's about reclaiming a sadly waning masculine autonomy in a world where, according to them, men are increasingly being failed, rejected, and marginalised.

Many MGTOW men feel disillusioned with societal norms that seem to favour women, especially in discussions around family law, education, and workplace dynamics. This discontent has created an environment where some men feel that the traditional roles they've been taught to aspire to – being a provider, a partner, a father – are no longer viable or rewarding. Instead, MGTOW offers an alternative: a life lived on one's own terms, free from what they perceive as the constraints imposed by women and societal expectations.

The MGTOW movement fosters a sense of distrust towards women and relationships, potentially leading to isolation for the men who fall for the movement's rhetoric. It's worrying to think about the implications of this: if young men fall for a MGTOW mindset, they may shy away from forming meaningful connections with women – romantic or otherwise – which could hinder their emotional and social development.

What MGTOWs don't realise is that positive relationships with the opposite sex are essential to men's good health. For example, a study looking at over 100,000 people across seven different countries found that people who were not married or in marriage-like romantic relationships were at greater risk of depression than people who were in married or cohabiting relationships.[17] This effect was particularly strong for men.

When it comes to platonic relationships, men get more emotional support and 'therapeutic value' from opposite-sex platonic relationships than they do with friends of the same sex.[18] If MGTOWs really cared about men's needs, then they'd be cultivating friendships with women rather than avoiding them.

Some of what you'll find in MGTOW spaces is, frankly, worrying. Certain corners of the movement don't just advocate independence from women – they paint women as the enemy. For those of us working in education, with a majority female workforce, this matters. We're trying to teach boys to build healthy relationships, to see strength in kindness, and to treat others and themselves with respect. The narratives pushed by MGTOW can cut right across that, making our job harder.

So, while MGTOW markets itself as male self-empowerment, there's a lot going on under the surface. And we can't afford to ignore it. As teachers, we need to understand where these ideas come from and how they seep into the thinking of the boys in front of us. We need to have these conversations, not just to challenge the negativity but to help boys find a version of masculinity that's healthy, balanced, and doesn't rely on putting others down. This stuff is on their radar. It needs to be on ours too.

Pick-Up Artists

There's a pub where, in the summer, the sun bounces off the surface of the River Thames, casting a light that dapples and dances across the faces of those sipping crisp, cold beers on the riverbank. In winter, a gigantic chandelier in the entrance draws gasps from people stepping in from the cold, all hoping to snag a seat by the huge open fire that warms frozen hands and fills cold noses with the comforting scent of woodsmoke.

It was one such winter, in 2006, when a group of women on a hen do came into that pub, ready to drink, laugh, and dance the night away. As the drinks flowed, so did the laughter. The place filled up around them, and one of the women, Sarah, noticed a table of three lads, about 18 or 19, glancing over and whispering to each other.

'What are you looking at?' Sarah called across to the young men, half-laughing.

The boys looked embarrassed. And it was that embarrassment that pushed one of the boys to approach their table a few minutes later.

'Sorry, ladies,' the boy stammered. 'We didn't mean to stare. We were just admiring how much fun you all seemed to be having. Honestly… we're gay, so you've got nothing to worry about from us.'

The hen do roared with laughter. Half an hour later, the women invited the boys over, and the night rolled on with drinks, dancing, and laughter. The women felt safe while the boys soaked up the attention of older female company. At the end of the night, amidst drunken goodbyes and well-intentioned promises to meet again, one of the boys turned to Sarah and said something that threw her off balance: 'You know what? I've never fancied a woman before, but you're different. I quite like you.'

'That's strange…' thought Sarah.

Strange indeed. Because that boy wasn't gay. He never had been. He was straight. Desperate. And dishonest. How do I know? Because that boy – that lying, manipulative boy – was me.

At 18, I'd try anything to get a woman's attention. Pretending to be gay? Just another tactic from the Pick-Up Artist (PUA) playbook.

Unmasking the Manosphere

PUA culture really found its moment in 2005, when journalist Neil Strauss published *The Game*, a book that chronicled his initiation into this world of manipulation and seduction. The book became a bestseller: a bible for men convinced that attraction was a science, a formula you could learn and execute with military precision.

PUAs believe that, with the right techniques, or *games*, any man can make himself sexually irresistible. At the core of this belief is a simple idea: women are drawn to power. Show dominance, control the interaction, and you can make them want you.

A key pillar of PUA thinking is the idea of the 'alpha male'. The alpha is confident, assertive, socially dominant. Add to that a carefully crafted, charismatic, playful persona, and you become magnetic.

A quick Google search will show you just how lucrative this has become: online and in-person PUA courses, charging hundreds of pounds or dollars, where young men are 'trained' by 'professional' PUAs with impressive 'body counts' (their term for the number of women they've slept with) as living proof that the system works.

One of the more notorious PUA seduction techniques is *negging*. A 'neg' is a backhanded compliment designed to chip away at a woman's self-esteem. Something like: *'Your hair's a nice colour, though it's a shame the style doesn't quite work with that dress.'* The theory is simple: undermine her confidence, elevate your own, and you suddenly become more powerful, and therefore more attractive, in her eyes.

Another staple of the PUA arsenal is *peacocking* – the act of dressing in outlandish clothes (think leopard print leggings or a ridiculous hat) to broadcast confidence and non-conformity. The message? *'I don't follow the rules. I make them.'*

The entire world of PUAs rests on the assumption that women are little more than programmable machines: insult them, confuse them, show dominance, and they'll fall into bed with you. In this worldview, women are not people. They're commodities. They exist to be consumed, conquered, and counted.

And here's the thing: it doesn't just degrade women. It deforms men, too. It teaches boys that connection comes through deceit. That power matters more than kindness. That manipulation is a skill to be honed.

I know. I was that boy once.

MRAs

Men's Rights Activism (MRA) is a movement focused on solving the so-called problems that men face in areas such as family law, education, mental health, and social pressures, and Men's Rights Activists (MRAs) have taken it upon themselves to stand up for the perceived inequalities that they believe men now face as a result of greater female empowerment. The titles of one popular MRA's TikTok posts read like a litany of male injustice: *Men are Not the Oppressors*; *End Sexism Against Men*; *No Happiness for Men*; *Women are Choosing to Believe that Men are Violent*; *How Many Men is 'All Men'?*

At the heart of MRA ideology is the belief that men are disadvantaged in a number of societal areas. They believe that when it comes to child custody and child support arrangements, the law favours mothers over fathers, which has a negative impact not only on the men who are allegedly being treated unfairly in these situations but also on the children who are left fatherless, or with restricted access to their fathers, as a result. A report from The Fathering Project does indicate that in households where a father or father figure is present, boys show reduced delinquency rates, as well as better developmental and educational outcomes.[19] However, the 'boys need fathers' argument is flawed in that it automatically assumes that all fathers are positive role models for their children. Ninety-three percent of defendants in domestic abuse cases are male: are

Unmasking the Manosphere

the men who are fathers in this group positive role models for their children just because they are men?

Despite rejecting claims of anti-feminism, many MRA belief systems are underpinned by resentment towards women. When it comes to education, MRAs believe that boys are being severely let down by a teaching profession made up of a predominantly female workforce. The Reddit thread r/MensRights contains a whole host of comments, blog posts, and videos in which the injustices male pupils face at the hands of female teachers are exposed. One post, 'Female Teacher-Student Sex is an EPIDEMIC', explains how female teachers are abusing male pupils. Comments from users are interesting: One user bemoans the fact that 'the nasty c*nts in a lot of cases could have gotten any man, but they chose to do such things'. Another post, titled 'Why are so many teachers sexist?' asks some important rhetorical questions: 'A boy and girl are arguing? Teacher tells the boy off? A girl hits a boy? Nothing.'

To be fair, not everything coming out of the MRA world is nonsense. There are real issues: male suicide rates, family court biases, and the pressure on men to be emotionally closed off. But alongside those genuine concerns sits a darker undercurrent: bitterness, resentment, and a narrative that often turns women into scapegoats. And that's where things can start to go very wrong for the boys and girls in our schools.

The MRA story is seductive. It tells boys: *'The world's rigged against you. Women have all the power. Don't trust them.'* It plays into old stereotypes of masculinity – that men must be strong, stoic, and silent. Vulnerability? Weakness. Asking for help? Weakness. Instead of encouraging boys to open up, it teaches them to close ranks and bottle everything up. We already know where that road leads: anxiety, depression, silence, and suffering.

On top of that, the constant rhetoric around false rape allegations – a common theme of MRA forums – can foster a warped sense of paranoia. Boys start to view girls not as friends, equals, or potential partners, but as threats. For girls, the fallout is just as toxic. When boys buy into the idea that women are the enemy, it creates a culture where girls feel less safe speaking out. The message is clear: *'Your pain doesn't matter. Your voice is part of the problem.'* That kind of climate doesn't just impact individual relationships; it shapes entire classroom dynamics and school cultures.

As teachers, we need to know this stuff. We need to talk about it, even if it feels uncomfortable. Yes, some MRA talking points are worth listening to – male mental health and fatherhood rights matter. But they need to be part of a bigger conversation about empathy, balance, and respect. Our job is to help boys and girls see each other as allies, not opponents. Because if we don't tackle these narratives in the classroom, the internet will do it for us. And the internet doesn't care about kindness.

What Schools and Teachers Can Do

The instinct, when faced with something as grim and unsettling as the incel subculture or MGTOW rhetoric, is often to hope that our boys won't find it. That they'll scroll past the forums and memes. That they'll know better. But hope is not a strategy.

If schools are serious about protecting boys from radicalisation, then they need to stop treating this as a fringe issue. Manosphere ideologies fill the vacuum left behind when boys feel voiceless, powerless, or confused about where they fit in. If we're not talking to boys about masculinity, someone else is.

Here's what schools can – and must – do.

1. Name the Manosphere

Let's stop skirting around it.

Unmasking the Manosphere

We can't protect boys from ideologies we never name. Too many schools feel nervous about saying words like *incel* or *PUA* in assemblies or lessons. But here's the thing: if a 13-year-old boy is watching a YouTuber who teaches 'negging' or says women 'hit the wall' at 30, he already knows these terms. Pretending otherwise just makes us look naive.

Instead, we should:

- Explicitly teach the difference between healthy masculinity and movements like MGTOW, incel forums, or men's rights groups
- Break down their language: explain what 'chad', 'beta', or 'AWALT' mean and why those beliefs are toxic
- Discuss real-world consequences: share how online misogyny can escalate into offline violence (e.g. Elliot Rodger, Jake Davison), or how it corrodes boys' ability to form respectful, loving relationships

We name racism. We name homophobia. We must name this too.

The boys being pulled into the Manosphere are not always the ones causing problems in class. Often, they're quiet. They do their homework. They sit at the back and stew. These boys don't need punishment – they need tools. We must teach boys how to analyse the content they see online with the same rigour we'd expect when they're evaluating a poem or a historical source. That means going beyond 'don't believe everything you see online' and helping them understand:

- How algorithms funnel extreme content
- How incel forums reward the most outrageous views with attention and status
- How 'data' about gender differences is often manipulated, misused, or taken from deeply flawed studies

- How 'us vs them' thinking is a hallmark of every radical movement, be it religious extremism or the Manosphere

Boys need to feel smart for spotting manipulation – not just ashamed for falling for it.

2. Give Boys a Place to Talk – And Be Heard

One of the Manosphere's most dangerous lies is that *only* these forums are telling boys the truth about women, dating, or power. To counter that, boys need somewhere they can be honest about what's bothering them. That includes things like:

- Rejection
- Loneliness
- Not feeling good enough
- Feeling ashamed of wanting connection, sex, or intimacy

Schools should create structured spaces where boys can talk about this stuff. Mentoring schemes, discussion groups, or even targeted PSHE sessions with male staff who can role-model vulnerability and strength can make a huge difference. But listening must come before lecturing. Boys won't open up if they think they'll be shut down.

3. Intervene Early

The signs of early-stage Manosphere radicalisation are often subtle. A boy who used to be kind suddenly mocking girls behind their back. Someone quoting 'biological truths' about why men are more logical. A quiet obsession with dating hierarchies or memes that treat women as gold-diggers or cheaters. Rather than dismiss this as 'just banter' or 'edgy humour', staff should be trained to spot these as possible warning signs.

Unmasking the Manosphere

This also means involving form tutors and subject teachers, not just safeguarding leads. The early signs don't always come out in RSE: they emerge in corridors, group chats, or the back row of maths.

4. Teach Boys That Caring Is Masculine

Much of the Manosphere is built on contempt: for women, yes – but also for empathy, compromise, softness. The antidote to that isn't just better arguments. It's *different role models*.

Schools should platform men who are:

- Emotionally intelligent
- Respectful of women without being performative
- Confident without dominating others
- Willing to admit mistakes, change views, and grow

Invite speakers in. Share videos or interviews. Use novels and non-fiction texts that portray these kinds of men. Build this into the curriculum, not just PSHE. And most of all: show boys, through school culture, that these traits are not just tolerated – they are *respected*.

5. Reject 'Boys Will Be Boys'

Lastly, and perhaps most importantly, schools must challenge the culture that enables all of this. The eyerolls when a boy makes a sexist joke. The silence when a girl is talked over. The excuses made for boys who 'struggle with boundaries'. Every time a school lets this go, it pushes boys one step closer to thinking the Manosphere might have a point.

But when we set high expectations – for respect, for kindness, for accountability – we give boys something far more valuable than a red pill: we give them a way out.

The Final Word

The Manosphere isn't some dark corner of the internet that boys stumble into by accident. It's loud, it's accessible, and it's actively recruiting – through memes, half-truths, and promises of belonging. If we're not giving boys connection, purpose, and healthy models of masculinity in our classrooms, someone else is going to do it for us – and that someone might be a bitter man in a basement, teaching them that women are the enemy and violence is power. We can't shy away from these conversations because they feel awkward. We need to be proactive, deliberate, and open. Boys need to know that vulnerability isn't weakness, that kindness isn't naivety, and that strength has nothing to do with dominance. If we don't shape that message, the Manosphere will.

Notes

1. Sugiura, L. (2021). *The incel rebellion: The rise of the Manosphere and the virtual war against women.* Emerald Group Publishing, p. 23.
2. www.gov.uk/government/statistics/individuals-referred-to-prevent-to-march-2024/individuals-referred-to-and-supported-through-the-prevent-programme-april-2023-to-march-2024#type-of-concern
3. https://medium.com/@worstonlinedater/tinder-experiments-ii-guys-unless-you-are-really-hot-you-are-probably-better-off-not-wasting-your-2ddf370a6e9a
4. www.oii.ox.ac.uk/news-events/new-study-reveals-changing-trends-in-online-dating/
5. www.npr.org/2014/09/06/345884282/online-dating-stats-reveal-a-dataclysm-of-telling-trends
6. www.science.org/doi/10.1126/sciadv.aap9815
7. www.bbc.co.uk/news/world-us-canada-45284455
8. Kalish, R., & Kimmel, M. (2010). Suicide by mass murder: Masculinity, aggrieved entitlement, and rampage school shootings. *Health Sociology Review, 19*(4), 451–464. https://doi.org/10.5172/hesr.2010.19.4.451
9. Moskalenko, S., Kates, N., González, J. F.-G., & Bloom, M. (2022). Predictors of radical intentions among incels: A survey of 54 self-identified incels. *Journal of Online Trust and Safety, 1*(3). https://doi.org/10.54501/jots.v1i3.57

10. *Predicting harm among incels (involuntary celibates): The roles of mental health, ideological belief and social networking (accessible)*. (n.d.). GOV.UK. www.gov.uk/government/publications/predicting-harm-among-incels-involuntary-celibates/predicting-harm-among-incels-involuntary-celibates-the-roles-of-mental-health-ideological-belief-and-social-networking-accessible#summary-and-conclusion
11. De Roos, M., Veldhuizen-Ochodničanová, L., & Hanna, A. (2024). The angry echo chamber: A study of extremist and emotional language changes in incel communities over time. *Journal of Interpersonal Violence, 39*(21–22). https://doi.org/10.1177/08862605241239451
12. www.itv.com/news/westcountry/2023-01-18/father-and-daughter-shot-dead-in-keyham-attack-were-found-cradling-each-other
13. www.theguardian.com/uk-news/2023/jan/18/plymouth-shooter-jake-davison-fascinated-by-mass-shootings-and-incel-culture-inquest-hears
14. Jaki, S., De Smedt, T., Gwóźdź, M., Panchal, R., Rossa, A., & De Pauw, G. (2019). Online hatred of women in the Incels.me forum: Linguistic analysis and automatic detection. *Journal of Language Aggression & Conflict, 7*(2), 240–268. https://doi.org/10.1075/JLAC.00026.JAK
15. Speckhard, A., Ellenberg, M., Morton, J., & Ash, A. (2021). Involuntary celibates' experiences of and grievance over sexual exclusion and the potential threat of violence among those active in an online incel forum. *Journal of Strategic Security, 14*(2), 89–121. https://doi.org/10.5038/1944-0472.14.2.1910
16. Sugiura, L. (2021). *The incel rebellion: The rise of the Manosphere and the virtual war against women*. Emerald Group Publishing, p. 27.
17. www.theguardian.com/lifeandstyle/2024/nov/04/moving-in-with-someone-cuts-chances-of-being-depressed-finds-study
18. Aukett, R., Ritchie, J., & Mill, K. (1988). Gender differences in friendship patterns. *Sex Roles, 19*(1–2), 57–66. https://doi.org/10.1007/BF00292464
19. https://thefatheringproject.org/engaging-fathers-in-a-non-violent-future/

2

Alpha Males, Algorithms, and Adult Content

How Influencers and Porn Are Warping Boyhood

From Manosphere to Mainstream

The dark, murky corners of the Manosphere aren't the only places where online misogyny thrives. Misogyny is also seeping into the online spaces we might consider 'mainstream'. Whether it's through TikTok clips, Instagram reels, YouTube Shorts, or group chats, many of the boys we teach are coming into regular, unfiltered content with anti-female online content that is legitimising displays of misogynistic attitudes and behaviours in the real world.

There are two forces in particular that are responsible for the damaging attitudes many boys are displaying: pornography, which teaches boys from an early age that sex is about the assertion of male power and domination over willingly submissive females, and toxic influencers, who sell misogyny as a means of obtaining female adoration. Together, they're shaping a warped version of masculinity that shows up not only in the online world but the 'real world' also.

The Impact of Pornography on Attitudes

Research from the Children's Commissioner, published in 2023, found that in the UK, the average age at which a child first saw pornography is 13 years old.[1] Of over 1,000 16 to 21-year-olds surveyed, 50% of young people had sought out pornography online, with boys being more likely to do so – 58% of boys had searched for pornography compared to 42% of girls. Males are much more likely to be frequent users of pornography, with 21% of 16 to 21-year-old males watching it at least once a day compared to just 7% of girls. The younger a person is when they first consume pornography, the more likely they are to become addicted.

The survey also asked 18 to 21-year-olds to answer questions based on their sexual experiences before the age of 18. The study describes how 'girls were significantly more likely to have experienced a violent sex act compared to boys', with nearly half (48%) of girls having experienced a violent sex act before the age of 18. Forty-seven per cent of those surveyed believed that girls *expect* sex to involve physical aggression, with 42% believing that girls enjoy physically aggressive sex acts.

It's perfectly reasonable to ascribe blame for these beliefs to pornography: content analyses of mainstream pornography tell us exactly what boys are learning. In 2010, a landmark study by Bridges et al. found that 88% of scenes in the top-selling porn videos contained physical aggression, almost always from men towards women.[2] The message is consistent and clear: sex is something men do to women. Consent is not a discussion point; domination and submission are the default.

Violence in Pornography

A content analysis study of over 4,000 heterosexual scenes from two of the biggest free porn platforms, Pornhub and Xvideos, gives us a disturbing snapshot of what many boys are consuming as their first introduction to sex.[3] The study found that nearly half of Pornhub's videos (45%) and over a third of Xvideo's material (35%) featured at least one act of physical aggression. Spanking, gagging, slapping, hair-pulling, and choking were the most common. In 97% of these scenes, the

Alpha Males, Algorithms, and Adult Content

aggression was directed at women, and overwhelmingly it was men enacting it. Crucially, the women's reactions were typically either neutral or positive – rarely was pain or distress shown. In other words, boys are being shown again and again that violence towards women is not just normal but welcomed. There is no pause. No consequence. No accountability. Just a quiet, relentless drip-feed of dominance as desire.

All that being said, there's no concrete evidence that watching violent porn on its own causes someone to go out and commit rape or sexual assault. Neil Malamuth, one of the world's leading experts on pornography, says that for most men, watching porn – even violent porn – doesn't make them more likely to act violently. For the small number who do watch porn and then go on to be sexually violent, other risk factors tend to be at play: a violent upbringing, narcissism, entitlement, or a history of being sexually abused themselves.

While watching porn might not turn boys into rapists, there's strong evidence that it shapes the way they see women. Research has shown that men who watch pornography are more likely to view women as sex objects, to try and replicate the sex they're seeing in pornography in their real-life sexual encounters, and to harbour sexually aggressive views towards women.[4]

When women and girls are viewed as objects, they tend to be treated as such, and the effects on them are extremely harmful: depression, eating disorders, sexual anxiety. Girls who grow up being objectified repeatedly pay a heavy psychological price.

Porn: Panic or Problem?

For many teenage boys, porn is not just entertainment. It's sex education, relationship guidance, and an unspoken script for how they think they're supposed to behave and how they think women are supposed to respond. Without proper education, boys may internalise the messages of male dominance observed in most pornography. A huge 2016 meta-analysis by Wright, Tokunaga, and Kraus confirmed what many adults suspect: frequent porn consumption is linked to greater acceptance of rape myths, reduced empathy for victims of sexual violence, and stronger beliefs in male dominance.[5]

In school corridors and classrooms, these beliefs leak out in unsettling ways. A boy half-laughing, half-curious, once asked me: *'Sir, is choking normal during sex?'* He wasn't trying to shock me: he just genuinely didn't know. For him, that was what intimacy looked like. That's what the world of online pornography had taught him before his first kiss.

When you combine these violent portrayals of male-on-female sex with the messages boys are absorbing from toxic male influencers who tell them that women are hypergamous, manipulative, and only respond to power, you start to see why resentment festers. If reality doesn't match the fantasy they've been sold, boys can feel short-changed. And that frustration quickly turns into entitlement: *I deserve this. Why won't they give it to me?*

Understandably, some teachers are reluctant to talk openly to students about porn. But by avoiding it, we leave the field wide open for the internet to do the talking, and, largely, the internet is not interested in respect, empathy, or consent.

I've heard boys use the phrase *'It's what they like though, isn't it?'* when describing acts that are inherently violent. And the weird thing is, not all boys who give voice to such questions are cruel or intentionally vile. Many of them are just confused. They're confused because they've been miseducated by a system that profits from their ignorance.

If teachers and parents don't step in to challenge these narratives carefully, sensitively, and firmly, then we are complicit in leaving

Alpha Males, Algorithms, and Adult Content

boys to learn about sex and relationships from a script written by profit-driven algorithms and studios that glamorise degradation. We're leaving them unprepared for real relationships, setting them up for frustration, misunderstanding, and, in some cases, aggression.

The Rise of Toxic Influencers

There was a time when boys who struggled with confidence, rejection, or loneliness dealt with it by writing bad poetry, creating a mixtape of heartbreak anthems, or learning songs on the guitar, badly, to play at a party where she was never going to be. Please don't ask me how I know this.

Today, it's different. Now, many boys' first port of call for solutions to their romantic failings is YouTube, TikTok, or Instagram. And the answers they're offered can be dangerous. Toxic male influencers like Andrew Tate, with their memeable soundbites, promise boys that they can be powerful, admired, and in control so long as they reject weakness and any notion that women are their equals. The mask is self-improvement; the reality is entitlement and misogyny.

Andrew Tate is only one fly on the turd. When you dig deeper, you have an entire network of Tate wannabes building platforms around the same formula: tap into male insecurity, promise dominance and success, and then blame women for everything that feels unfair. On the surface, it's all about productivity and purpose; scratch beneath, and you find the same old story: women as obstacles or commodities, and masculinity defined by control and conquest.

Why do these toxic influencers, or 'alpha bros' as they're sometimes called, resonate so deeply with teenage boys? They resonate because teenage boys are at a vulnerable crossroads: they are desperate to feel confident and valued. They're trying to understand where they fit in a world that often feels confusing and critical of men. And the social media algorithms serve these messages up before boys

Unmasking the Manosphere

even know what they're looking for. A single search for 'how to be more confident' or 'how to talk to girls' can spiral into a feed filled with alpha male dogma and content that normalises resentment and entitlement.

A recent study by Dublin City University's Anti-Bullying Centre has revealed just how aggressively social media algorithms push misogynistic and male supremacist content onto young male users.[6] The research team set up ten 'sock puppet' accounts on blank smartphones (five on YouTube Shorts and five on TikTok) to track the kind of content served up to male-identified users.

The results are deeply concerning. Regardless of whether these accounts actively searched for misogynistic material or not, on average it took just 23 minutes before the accounts were recommended anti-feminist, masculinist, and extremist content. And once engagement began, the problem escalated fast. By the time each phone had consumed around 400 videos (roughly two to three hours of viewing), most of the content recommended was toxic: 76% of videos were toxic on TikTok, with 78% of videos considered toxic on YouTube Shorts. Most of this came from the Manosphere and consisted of videos pushing alpha male posturing, anti-feminism, and calls for the submission of women.

In schools, we see the symptoms of engaging with online misogynistic content: boys parroting influencer catchphrases, treating casual misogyny as edgy banter, testing boundaries with jokes that aren't really jokes. Often, they don't even realise how these ideas have taken root – they just know it feels good to belong to something. It feels good to stop blaming themselves for their social awkwardness or romantic disappointments and, instead, direct that blame elsewhere.

The worrying part is that these toxic influencers are constantly evolving. By the time you read this, Andrew Tate may be consigned to irrelevancy. Instead, there'll be new faces on TikTok and YouTube

Alpha Males, Algorithms, and Adult Content

offering the same poison as Tate, albeit in slightly different packaging. That's why it's not enough to name and shame the big players; we must help boys understand the tactics, the manipulation, and the emotional hooks that make this content so appealing. We have to teach them to spot the trap before they fall into it. Because if we don't, the internet will be more than happy to do the teaching for us.

The Impact of Influencers on Attitudes

In 2023, Women's Aid published the findings of their report, *Influencers and attitudes: How will the next generation understand domestic abuse?*[7] The report surveyed 1,000 young people aged between 7 and 18, and, among other things, focused on the impact that toxic male influencer Andrew Tate had on young people's attitudes towards issues such as sex, consent, and gender-based violence.

Those who come across 'AT content' – the phrase used in the report to refer to not only Tate's content but also other misogynistic content found online – were much more likely to agree with toxic ideas about relationships. For example, almost a third (31%) of those exposed to AT content believed that every relationship needs one person in the relationship to be in control. For those that hadn't consumed AT content this figure dropped to 14%.

Thirty-five per cent of those who'd seen AT content thought that 'love bombing' – the process by which someone overwhelms another person with excessive attention early on in a relationship in order to gain control or create dependence – is romantic. For those who haven't been exposed to AT content, only 13% saw that behaviour as acceptable, all of which goes to show the way toxic online influencers dress coercive and controlling behaviours up as devotion.

Most worryingly, nearly one in five (19%) of the children and young people who'd seen AT content said it's okay to hurt someone physically as long as you apologise afterwards. This is compared to the 4% of those who'd not seen AT content. In other words, exposure to AT content made young people almost *five times* more likely to believe hitting someone is okay so long as you say sorry.

In 2023, YouGov published findings that showed one in eight boys aged 6–15 agreed with Andrew Tate's views on women.[8] Given that these views include the idea that rape victims must 'bear responsibility' for the horrific crimes inflicted upon them by men, and that violence against a woman who accuses you of cheating is acceptable, this should be of huge concern.[9]

Teachers cannot afford to ignore this. We cannot assume that boys will simply grow out of it. The messages that the dual toxic influences of online misogynistic influencers and pornography give out are loud, repetitive, and dangerously seductive. If teachers and parents do not offer an alternative narrative – one rooted in empathy, respect and genuine strength – then the toxic areas of the internet will.

What's Happening in Schools?

Some people assume that sexual abuse and misogyny is a predominantly secondary school problem, but the truth is that students as young as five or six are being sexually harassed by their peers at primary school. As of 2025, 1,664 primary schools were listed on the *Everyone's Invited* website as places where sexual abuse and harassment had occurred. The testimonies are harrowing and make for difficult reading:

> I was assaulted when I was in year four by my peers at school. We played 'it' in the in the playground then one of the boys said that we should go into the toilet and play in there so I did when I went in I locked the doors so they couldn't get in and it was just me and two other guys one of them grabbed me from behind

and started humping me then he took his trousers off and did things to me. Primary.[10]

I was in year two at a primary school in [location omitted to preserve anonymity]. It was a male peer, someone I thought was my friend. He was always with me at school and followed me everywhere. I remember him always grabbing and touching me, but I didn't know I could say I didn't like it. One day, he exposed his penis to me at school and wanted me to touch it. He kept asking and pushing, grabbing my hand. He only stopped when a teacher appeared, and the bell went. I don't know if the teacher saw anything, but they didn't do anything. I never told anyone as I didn't know it was wrong. It's my earliest memory of my life.

When I was in year 2 or 3, there was a boy in my class who seemed like a nice person. We were good friends. One day, he asked me to follow him to the unisex bathrooms at break time/playtime. Since I was like 7 and absolutely clueless, I did. He told me to close my eyes, and he proceeded to pull down my trousers and pants and lick/kiss my private areas in an incredibly sexual manner. I didn't like it but I never spoke up.[11]

As noted in the introduction, the problem continues into secondary school, where 92% of secondary age girls report hearing sexist name-calling a lot or sometimes, with 79% of girls saying sexual assault happens a lot or often.[12]

Misogyny isn't always from a place of malintent. I remember visiting a school to speak to students about sexual harassment. During the session we'd discussed how commenting on the way people look or dress and making assumptions about their sexual behaviour as a result is sexual harassment. At the end of the session, I remember a boy raised his hand and very politely, and without any trace of deliberate provocation, asked me: *'So if my girlfriend wears something I don't want her to wear and I ask her to change, is that sexual harassment?'* I explained to him that this sort of request would be deemed as coercive control – any one of a pattern of behaviours used to dominate, isolate, or intimidate someone, often without physical violence. Other examples of coercive control could include monitoring or checking someone's phone or making them feel guilty for spending time with others. The boy looked at me with complete shock, before asking, with audible surprise: *'So even though she's mine, if she's wearing something that shows off too much of her body, I can't say anything?'* I replied in the negative and he thanked me for answering his question, before turning to face his friends, head shaking in disbelief. Often, when I talk to boys, they ask me questions with the deliberate intention of provoking me or asserting their own misogyny. This boy? His question was genuine and well intentioned, as was his disbelief at the fact that he, an 11-year-old boy, shouldn't assume that his girlfriend is 'his' or that he should have any control as to how she presents herself to the world.

What Can Schools and Teachers Do?

None of this is easy. We're up against billion-pound industries, algorithmic rabbit holes, and influencers with more followers than the population of most European countries. But schools still count. Teachers still count. We could be the last line of defence against bad information and the people who tell boys that they're only valuable when they're dominant, detached, or dangerous. Here's what we can do:

1. Build Critical Thinkers

Critical thinking refers to the ability to think clearly and rationally using logic to inform opinion. It tends to involve questioning as a means of obtaining evidence and different perspectives, enabling the critical thinker to evaluate information and arguments before coming to an informed opinion.

Alpha Males, Algorithms, and Adult Content

If boys are being taught masculinity through algorithms, we must teach them how algorithms work. We can't just tell them that their social media feeds are curated but need to tell them how they're curated, and why.

Once they understand that a single search or click can drag them into an echo chamber, they're more likely to pause before assuming that what they see is what everyone sees. We can teach them to spot manipulation tactics: how influencers frame problems, offer simple (often sexist) solutions, and build parasocial trust to sell harmful ideas – or merchandise.

We must encourage boys to question the scripts they're being given. When they hear phrases like 'high value male' or 'women only want money', we need to help them interrogate that. Who benefits from that narrative? What's being sold? What's being lost?

Dr Nic Ponsford is an expert at asking questions to students. As founder of the Global Equality Collective, an online diversity platform dedicated to helping schools build cultures where everybody feels included, Ponsford asks students questions all the time to better understand their wants and needs. Usefully, she also used to be a Media Studies teacher with a special interest in gender representation. Ponsford recommends encouraging students to ask the following questions when engaging with misogynistic content online. Perhaps you, the teacher, could print them out on a sheet and give them to students as a prompt. Alternatively, why not select –with obvious caution (perhaps make your own parody) – and watch some online content in class and direct these questions to the students?

- **Who do you think this video is aimed at? Why?** *(Potential answer: It's being aimed at young men in order to get them to subscribe to the influencer's website)*
- **How does the speaker try to seem powerful or trustworthy? Is the version of masculinity shown realistic? Is it respectful?** *(Potential*

answer: The speaker is citing statistics without mentioning where they come from. He's surrounded by beautiful women and dressed in expensive jewellery. He's ignoring the women and has them on display, as if they're objects to be shown off)

- **How do you feel watching this? Why might they want you to feel that way?** *(Potential answer: I feel quite inspired by what the speaker is saying about masculinity. He might want me to feel this way so I sign up to one of his online courses)*
- **What seems missing or suspicious in what they're saying?** *(Potential answer: Although he's talking a lot about what women think or feel, his videos never actually show women giving their opinion. And even if they did, how do I know the women aren't simply reading off his script?)*
- **What beliefs or values are being promoted here? Are they helpful or harmful? How are they being constructed or represented?** *(Potential answer: He's saying that there's no such thing as a gender pay gap. He's stating everything as fact, without telling me where he gets his evidence from. This could be harmful as it may be misleading)*
- **Would these views be acceptable at school/work? Why or why not? Who is the audience and how is the message framed? What is the impact of this on the consumer?** *(Potential answer: He's saying that rape should be legalised. There's no way you could say this at work as it would probably get you in a lot of trouble. He's aiming this message at men and saying that legalised rape is something women would be grateful for as they like it when men take control. This could be a very damaging message, particularly to naive, gullible, or impressionable young teens like some of my peers)*
- **Is this influencer using tactics like fear or shame? What's the effect?** *(Potential answer: This man is saying that there's no such thing as male depression and that men who cry are weak. He doesn't know this for fact. Neither do I. This could potentially shame men who struggle with negative emotions)*

Alpha Males, Algorithms, and Adult Content

- **What could be the impact of watching content like this often?** *(Potential answer: If I keep watching pornographic content like this, it could affect the way I view women)*
- **Why might algorithms boost this content?** *(Potential answer: This video may be being recommended to me by the algorithm because this social media platform knows that the more people who watch it, the more advertising money they receive)*
- **Whose stories or voices are not shown in this video?** *(Potential answer: This video is talking a lot about rape victims but gives no voice to a woman who has actually been raped)*
- **What version of masculinity is being sold? Who benefits from it?** *(Potential answer: This version of masculinity doesn't value women. The people who benefit from this are men but at the cost of women's happiness)*
- **What persuasive tactics are at play?** *(Potential answer: He's using lots of statistics, but he's not telling us where these are from. How do we know they're not just made up?)*
- **Why are vulnerable young men drawn to this content? What gaps are being exploited?** *(Potential answer: This man is claiming that he can teach young men to make any woman fall for him. This would be an attractive idea to men who haven't yet found love or had sex. He's exploiting their loneliness in order to cash in)*

2. Talk About Porn

The content flooding boys' algorithms doesn't stop at misogynistic sound bites. It extends into graphic, often violent online pornography, and the line between the two is thinner than many adults realise. When a boy watches a podcast clip where a misogynistic influencer talks about 'putting women in their place' and then later sees a porn scene in which a woman is being dominated or degraded, the message is consistent and dangerous: sex is a time for women to be controlled rather than cared for.

Unmasking the Manosphere

It's important we give boys alternative narratives on the subject of sex. If we're not teaching them what real intimacy looks like, what consent *actually* means, and how emotional connection and mutual pleasure work, then we leave it to the internet to educate them on sex.

PJ Livett is a national award-winning relationships and sex education expert and spends much of her time talking to young people about consent, pornography, and sex. When I spoke to her about the impact of pornography on boys, she stressed the importance of talking to boys about these things:

> When we create space for boys to talk openly about consent, boundaries, and their own experiences, we help dismantle harmful stereotypes and reduce the stigma around speaking up. It also empowers them to call out toxic or abusive behaviour, whether they witness it or experience it themselves, and to support others in doing the same.

This is all well and good but talking to young people about sex isn't easy. Luckily for us, Livett knows a thing or two:

> By creating safe, thoughtful spaces for conversations about sex and pornography, we can help young boys grow into young men who think critically, relate respectfully, and feel confident in a version of masculinity that lifts everyone up.

PJ LIVETT'S TIPS FOR TALKING TO BOYS ABOUT SEX AND PORNOGRAPHY

1. **Don't panic! You don't need to be a 'sexpert'...**
   Respond with curiosity, not judgement. You don't need to have all the answers. If a boy comes to you with a question, thank them. Remember, it's a privilege when they choose *you* to talk to. If he says something troubling,

try: *'That's interesting, where did you come across that?'* or *'How do you think that would feel if it happened to you or your friend?'*

2. **Create a judgement-free zone.**

   Let them know they won't be punished or shamed for being honest. The goal is understanding, not catching them out.

3. **Acknowledge curiosity is normal.**

   Let them know it is okay to be curious about sex. Normalise it. Say something like *'It's totally normal to want to understand your body, desire, and other people, it's just part of growing up.'*

4. **Debunk the 'performance' myth.**

   Help boys understand that porn actors are just that, actors. They are performing, not showing real-life sex, and are paid to make it look like 'real-life sex'. Emphasise that pleasure, vulnerability, awkwardness, and consent are all part of real connection.

5. **Distancing technique: Use media as a conversation starter.**

   If you see/hear something in a film, song, TV show, or ad that relates to sex or relationships, use it as a springboard: *'What do you think that's saying about men/women/relationships/sex? Think about the hidden messages: "What am I being sold?"'*

6. **Always be available for teens to talk to.**

   Teenagers want to talk about their concerns and experiences. If you are there for the little things, they are more likely to come to you with the big things. We wouldn't expect a teenager to sit their maths GCSE exams without teaching them about all the different elements of maths study, yet there is often a reluctance to help young people understand how to build and maintain healthy relationships and understand their bodies. Relationships and sex are intrinsically linked to a person's emotional, physical, social, and mental wellbeing. An understanding of human anatomy can help with safeguarding and boundaries and ultimately contribute towards establishing positive, healthy, safe relationships and sexual experiences.

7. **Start early and stay open.**

    Think of it as a 'slow-cooker approach' rather than 'microwave cooking': it's a gradual process, not instant. It's like scaffolding. Build up their 'knowledge bank' little and often. Ask questions about what they are seeing and hearing online. Invite conversation rather than shutting it down. It's better to have 100 one-minute conversations than to have one 100-minute conversation.

8. **Talk about values.**

    Use real-life situations to explore empathy, consent, and respect – not as a lecture but as a dialogue. Help them to think about what *they* value and therefore want in their ideal friendship/relationship.

9. **Help them understand the online world.**

    Teach them how algorithms work and why certain content gets pushed more than others.

10. **Offer positive role models.**

    Show examples of men who lead with kindness, integrity, and respect – not just confidence or popularity.

How Do You Know If a Person Has an Addiction to Porn?

Some of the signs:

- Interrupts thinking through the day/distracted/can't focus

- When viewing porn, moves from 'exploration' to 'dependency' (can't sleep without watching it first)
- Using porn to medicate a lot of emotions, pressures, or trauma
- They stop seeing friends and become more withdrawn, have only 'loose' connections with others
- They have no energy to do anything else and they're constantly chasing that high

What to Do If Somebody Comes to You and Confides in You...

- This is a real privilege. They have chosen YOU. Avoid using judgemental or shaming statements.
- Be sensitive in your approach – treat the other person as you would want to be treated. Be discreet, don't talk about it publicly, and be kind.
- Make sure they know that you're there for them – help them put boundaries in place and to be accountable.
- Signpost to organisations for further support, i.e. https://nakedtruthproject.com, which supports both the user and the partner of the user.

The simple fact is that young people are waking up every day looking for answers. But so often they are turning to pornography, or their peers, for their education.

What boys need most is not censorship but guidance. When we offer them connection over control, they are more likely to come to us with their deeper questions – not just about sex but about self-worth, respect, love, and identity.

Whether we're parents/carers, educators, or youth workers, we need to meet young people where they are. That means

> understanding the digital spaces they live in and creating safe, judgement-free opportunities to talk openly about sex, relationships, values, and boundaries. Because the messages they're getting from the world are loud and constant, it is up to us to offer something more grounded, more nuanced, and more human…
>
> PJ Livett

3. Address Incel Ideology Head-On

Incel ideology isn't just about forums and buzzwords. At its core, it's about boys feeling unwanted, unloved, and powerless – and being told that the only answer is hatred. We need to equip adults working in schools to understand the warning signs of radicalisation.

> *Children at risk of radicalisation may:*
> - Have low self-esteem
> - Be conflicted about their faith, identity, or sense of belonging
> - Be victims of bullying or discrimination
> - Feel isolated or lonely
> - Be experiencing stress or depression
> - Be going through a transitional period in their life
> - Be angry at other people or the government
> - Feel a sense of injustice at how people or society treats them
>
> *Indicators that a child may be being radicalised include:*
> - Withdrawal from family and friends
> - Increased hostility towards others

Alpha Males, Algorithms, and Adult Content

- Talking as if from a script
- Being unwilling to discuss their views
- Open expression of extremist viewpoints
- Increased levels of anger
- Secrecy
- Using language related to extreme groups or viewpoints, e.g. *Red Pill*
- Supporting violence and terrorism towards other cultures or nationalities, or supporting religious-based grievances
- Writing or creating artwork that promotes extremist values
- Possession of extremist alliteration
- Possession of any material relating to weapons, explosives, or military training

Adapted from www.bhscp.org.uk/people-working-with-children/radicalisation-extremism-and-the-prevent-duty/

Why not share information from the previous chapter on incels with staff in a training session? You could select key Manosphere vocabulary to give to staff to help them be vigilant in spotting inappropriate language that could signify incel-related radicalisation.

We also need to make boys feel connected to the school community and us, their teachers. We need to create spaces where they can talk openly about loneliness, rejection, and heartbreak, so that when they experience these things, it is us they come to, rather than the Manosphere and the toxic communities within it. Not every boy who's rejected becomes radicalised. But every boy who *is* radicalised was once just someone who felt ignored. Here's a few suggestions as to how we can foster a sense of connection between boys and the school community:

- **Notice the quiet ones.** Check in regularly with boys who seem withdrawn, isolated, or 'fine' on the surface, especially those not causing trouble. Quiet does not always mean content.
- **Validate emotional experiences.** Let boys know it's okay to feel anxious, sad, or rejected. Use neutral moments such as after class or during tutor time to normalise talking about feelings without making it a big deal.
- **Ask after them.** A quick 'How are you getting on?', a comment about something they're interested in, or praise for effort can build trust over time. Ask how they are and ask twice. The first answer they give won't always be the truthful one.
- **Be flexible with definitions of success.** Academic and sporting achievement aren't the only ways boys can be successful. Celebrate kindness, creativity, teamwork, personal growth, and displays of vulnerability.
- **Use groupings that mix social circles.** In lessons or activities, gently disrupt rigid social hierarchies so that isolated or unpopular boys don't stay on the margins.
- **Create safe spaces.** Set up safe lunchtime or after-school drop-ins (e.g. 'open chat room' or 'boys' talk circle') where boys can come, talk, or just be. Don't pressure them to share, but encourage everybody to listen.
- **Share your own humanity.** People often worry about teachers showing their emotions or letting a bit of their authentic self show, as if it's going to turn into some sort of laid-bare therapy session. But actually, when appropriate, showing that adults have felt rejection, made mistakes, or struggled too really helps boys to recognise vulnerability as a strength, not weakness.
- **Model positive masculinity.** Whether you're male or female staff, be deliberate in praising boys when they show empathy, openness, or courage in emotionally honest ways.

- **Watch out for online mimicry.** If a boy parrots influencer slogans or ideas, resist the urge to mock or demean, however tempting it might be! Instead, explore it. *'Interesting you said that — what do you think he meant by it?'* opens a dialogue, not a defence.
- **Partner with pastoral and SEN teams.** Some boys struggling socially may also have undiagnosed needs or face issues at home. Work with colleagues to build a wider safety net.
- **Give boys roles of responsibility.** Prefect roles, mentoring younger students, or involvement in student voice projects give boys a sense of purpose and belonging.

4. Celebrate Alternative Masculinities

We cannot keep talking about what boys *shouldn't* be without also celebrating what they *can* be. That means showing them men who lead with kindness, not control. Who are emotionally intelligent. Who are creative, curious, generous. From artists and activists to dads, teachers, brothers, and best mates. This also means diversifying the curriculum. Don't just teach the 'great men of history' who led through war. Introduce them to poets, peacemakers, and pioneers of progress. Let them read stories where boys are vulnerable. Let them see masculinity that isn't toxic.

5. Engage Parents

To protect boys and girls effectively, we need a *whole-community* response. That means spotting the signs early, creating support systems in school, and engaging parents so they can be allies, not bystanders, in this work.

Most parents *want* to help – they're just unsure how. Many don't know what Andrew Tate has said, or how algorithms work, or how quickly a child's feed can fill with violent, degrading content. And even if they do suspect something's wrong, the topic of porn or misogyny is often too awkward or intimidating to tackle at home.

Unmasking the Manosphere

Ways to Engage and Support Parents:

- **Run dedicated parent workshops or info evenings.** Focus on topics like: 'Understanding the Online World of Teen Boys', 'Talking to Your Son about Porn', or 'How Influencer Culture Is Shaping Masculinity'. Bring in outside experts if needed to lend authority and ease teacher pressure.
- **Send out clear, jargon-free guidance.** Use newsletters, school websites, or handouts to explain key terms (e.g. 'red pill', 'alpha male', 'black pill'), what the risks are, and how to spot early signs of radicalisation or porn exposure.
- **Offer conversation starters.** Give parents the language to open sensitive topics with their children:
    o 'Have you seen anything online that made you feel uncomfortable?'
    o 'Some people online talk about men needing to dominate women – what do you think about that?'
    o 'Do you think what you see in porn is realistic?'
    You could also provide students with the list of critical thinking questions provided earlier on.
- **Normalise parental involvement in online lives.** Encourage parents to *co-view* content, check recommended feeds together, and discuss what they're both seeing not as surveillance, but shared curiosity. Frame it as digital literacy rather than policing.
- **Create a parent resource bank.** Include links to trusted sites like CEOP, ThinkUKnow, Internet Matters, and The School of Sexuality Education. Curate YouTube videos, TED Talks, and short explainers about porn literacy and influencer culture.
- **Be clear about the school's stance.** If a child expresses support for misogynistic influencers or uses language drawn from incel ideology, parents should be informed compassionately. They need to understand that it's a safeguarding concern, not just 'boys being boys'.
- **Encourage shared responsibility, not shame.** Reassure parents: they're not bad parents because their child came across Andrew

Alpha Males, Algorithms, and Adult Content

Tate or watched porn. What matters is how they *respond*. Avoid finger-pointing and focus on solutions.

By actively involving parents, we strengthen our chances of reaching boys who are being quietly influenced at home. Schools can't monitor every phone, every feed, or every private group chat, but with parents on side, we have a far better shot at protecting and guiding the boys who are still working out what kind of men they want to become.

6. Create Counter-Narratives

If toxic masculinity is a story boys are being sold, we need to tell a better one. Use assemblies, tutor time, and enrichment sessions to model healthy relationships. Showcase examples of men who succeed without belittling others. Tell stories of courage that don't involve fists. Let boys hear, over and over again, that respect, vulnerability, and empathy aren't weaknesses. They're the core of being human. Because if we want to change what boys believe, we have to change what boys see, hear, and experience. That starts with us.

The Final Word

The internet is not going away. Influencers will keep talking. Porn will keep streaming. Algorithms will keep learning. But we can learn too. And so can the boys in our classrooms. We can help them learn to pause, to question, to feel, to connect. We can remind them that masculinity isn't something you have to prove by dominating others – it's something you define through the choices you make. The battle against toxic online content isn't about censorship or panic; it's about education, empathy, and presence. If we want to raise boys who are safe, kind, and self-assured, then we must be louder, wiser, and more consistent than the voices trying to pull them in the opposite direction. The future of masculinity is still being written and although it may feel at times as though our grip is loosening, teachers are holding the pen.

Notes

1. Children's Commissioner for England. (2023, January 31). *"A lot of it is actually just abuse" – Young people and pornography.*
2. Bridges, A. J., Wosnitzer, R., Scharrer, E., Sun, C., & Liberman, R. (2010). Aggression and sexual behavior in best-selling pornography videos: A content analysis update. *Violence Against Women*, 16(10), 1065–1085. https://doi.org/10.1177/1077801210382866
3. Fritz, N., Malic, V., Paul, B., & Zhou, Y. (2020). A descriptive analysis of the types, targets, and relative frequency of aggression in mainstream pornography. *Archives of Sexual Behavior*, 49(8), 3041–3053. https://doi.org/10.1007/s10508-020-01773-0
4. Government Equalities Office. (2021, January 15). *The relationship between pornography use and harmful sexual attitudes and behaviours: Literature review.*
5. Wright, P. J., Tokunaga, R. S., & Kraus, A. (2016). A meta-analysis of pornography consumption and actual acts of sexual aggression in general population studies. *Journal of Communication*, 66(1), 183–205. https://doi.org/10.1111/jcom.12201
6. Baker, C., Ging, D., & Andreasen, M. B. (2024, April). *Recommending toxicity: The role of algorithmic recommender functions on YouTube Shorts and TikTok in promoting male supremacist influencers* (Summary Report). DCU Anti-Bullying Centre, Dublin City University.
7. Women's Aid Federation of England. (2023). *Influencers and attitudes: How will the next generation understand domestic abuse?*
8. https://yougov.co.uk/society/articles/47419-one-in-six-boys-aged-6-15-have-a-positive-view-of-andrew-tate
9. www.theguardian.com/technology/2022/aug/06/andrew-tate-violent-misogynistic-world-of-tiktok-new-star
10. 'It' is another name for the childhood game 'tag'.
11. www.everyonesinvited.uk/primary/read
12. www.gov.uk/government/publications/review-of-sexual-abuse-in-schools-and-colleges/review-of-sexual-abuse-in-schools-and-colleges

3 Sexual Harassment in Schools and What to Do About It

When working with younger pupils on the topic of misogyny, I tell them that misogyny is when we treat or dislike women and girls unfairly, just because they're female. The reality is that it's a little more complex than that: it can be a hatred of women. A fear of women. A lack of trust in women. Most of the time, it's a complex intermingling of all of these things. However we want to define it, what it always looks like is a lack of respect for women.

Misogyny can manifest itself in many ways. Sometimes it can look like simply not listening to women's voices. I cringe when I think of the number of times I've witnessed a female colleague ask a male pupil to do something – tuck in his shirt, perhaps – only for him to completely ignore her, and then when I, or another male colleague, asks him to do the same thing, he does it immediately. At other times it can look like objectification, sexist jokes, and sometimes even sexual violence like rape and sexual assault. For me, one of the most insidious ways misogyny shows up in schools is through sexual harassment. I don't just mean extreme, headline-grabbing cases, but casual, everyday incidents: the comments, the 'banter', the looks, and the touches that so often go unchallenged. As someone who's worked in and visited hundreds of schools across the country, I've seen how corrosive this type of misogyny can be. It's toxic not because it is necessarily more serious than acts of sexual violence, but because everyday incidences of sexual harassment are where rape culture begins. When casual sexual harassment is normalised or ignored, it sends a message: this behaviour is acceptable here. And once that message takes root, the leap from sexual harassment to sexual assault and sexual violence becomes shorter than many would like to believe.

Rape Culture

In my introduction, I mentioned how back in 2019, I wrote in *BDT?* that British schools are 'laying the foundations of rape culture Britain'. There are slight variations on the available definitions of rape culture depending on where you look, but the following features can be useful in helping us to understand exactly what a rape culture looks like.

A rape culture is any society that:

- Blames victims of rape for what's happened to them. (*'She was flaunting herself. She wanted it!'*)
- Trivialises sexual assault (*'Boys will be boys!'*)
- Tolerates sexual harassment
- Defines manhood as sexually dominant and womanhood as sexually passive
- Puts pressure on men to be sexually experienced
- Puts pressure on women to give in to men's sexual advances
- Assumes only promiscuous women are raped
- Assumes that men do not get raped
- Does not take rape accusations seriously
- Declares rape allegations as false
- Teaches women to avoid being raped rather than teaching men not to rape

Sexual Harassment in Schools and What to Do About It

Rape Culture in Schools

The elements of rape culture are often found in schools:

1. **Victim Blaming**
   A 2016 report by Rape Crisis South London and the Rape and Sexual Abuse Support Centre found that of the 70 young people aged 13–16 they surveyed, 26% believed rape only happens because of the way women dress and act, or how much they drink.[1] 54% of respondents believed women and girls lie about being raped, either as an act of revenge or an attempt to garner sympathy.
2. **Trivialisation of Sexual Assault**
   'Boys will be boys!'
   Still one of the most dangerous phrases in education. It's used to brush off physical harassment. To dismiss persistent comments. To excuse grabbing, groping, or pressuring. I know of schools where boys have sexually assaulted girls and the response has been a stern word and a reminder about 'respecting each other'. In some cases, the victim is moved to another class, but the boy stays put. If that's not trivialising sexual assault, I don't know what is.
3. **Tolerates Sexual Harassment**
   As we've seen in the introduction, data from UK Feminista that says of the girls who have been sexually harassed during their time at secondary school, just 14% reported it to a teacher. That means 86% didn't: 86% of girls have learned to tolerate the sexual harassment inflicted upon them.
4. **Defines Manhood as Sexually Dominant and Womanhood as Sexually Passive**
   Boys who have lots of sex are 'players', while girls who do the same are labelled as 'slags' or 'sluts'. The rules of sex are set early: boys must want sex. They must pursue it. Girls must be chased and resist, but not too much. It's a dangerous script where boys feel pressure to perform, and girls feel pressure to comply.

5. **Puts Pressure on Men to Be Sexually Experienced**

    There is immense pressure on boys to have had sex. A 2003 report found that one in three boys aged 15–17 felt pressured to have sex compared to 23% of girls.[2] But it's not just sex: I've heard boys boast about masturbation and how often they do it, how much porn they watch. I've even heard boys competing with one another to name as many unusual sex positions or kinks as they can.

6. **Puts Pressure on Women to Give in to Men's Sexual Advances**

    A 2021 report into children's experience of sexual harassment in schools found that 'most girls say that boys asking for nude photographs of them is a regular occurrence and speak about the *constant* [my emphasis] pressure from boys to send photographs'. Girls who don't send nudes to their boyfriends are accused of being 'boring' or 'frigid' while those who do are often teased for being a 'slut' when the picture is shared around the school.[3] This pressure to send nudes may seem relatively normal for children, but it says a lot about a society where girls are not only expected to give naked pictures to men, but their bodies too.

7. **Assumes Only Promiscuous Women Are Raped**

    When girls report sexual violence, people still ask: *'What was she wearing?' 'Had she been drinking?' 'Why did she go back to his house?'* These questions don't come from bad people. They come from a culture that quietly believes *'good girls'* are safe, and *'bad girls'* invite danger. Schools often don't challenge this framing. Sometimes they reinforce it by policing girls' clothing via uniform policies that punish girls for wearing short skirts more than boys' behaviour.

8. **Assumes That Men Do Not Get Raped**

    This is still one of the least discussed issues in schools. Boys can be victims, but few ever say it because the stigma is crushing. Disclosure means risking humiliation, disbelief, and accusations of weakness. We talk about safeguarding, but how many boys feel safe enough to say *'Something happened to me'*? Until we address this silence, male survivors stay invisible and alone.

Two Forms of Sexual Harassment in Schools

Rape culture in schools manifests itself in two ways. First, child-on-child sexual harassment and abuse: sexualised comments in corridors, photos shared without consent, groping in crowded lunch queues. But there's also another, less discussed form that deserves just as much attention: the sexual harassment and abuse directed at teachers, particularly women teachers. Too often, teachers are the victims of inappropriate sexualised language. Sometimes this can be a clumsy, but no less inappropriate or intimidating, attempt at flirting from the perpetrators, but other times it can be far worse: deliberate efforts to make teachers feel dehumanised, threatened, scared, or uncomfortable. As well as inappropriate language, teachers – just like students – can also be victims of physical sexual assault.

Child-on-Staff Sexual Harassment and Abuse

I invited women teachers to tell me about their experiences of sexual harassment in schools. Here's a selection of the stories (names have been changed):

> *When I first started teaching, I co-taught a challenging class, the majority of whom were boisterous lads. One day, one of them stuck his ruler up my colleague's backside. She had a skirt on and literally, the ruler penetrated her. When she tried to get him sanctioned, she was totally unsupported. They told her he hadn't meant to do it and that it was to be expected of a 13-year-old boy. This boy had literally shoved a thirty-centimetre ruler inside of my colleague and nothing was done about it.*
>
> Justine

Unmasking the Manosphere

I had a Year 8 student say out loud and within earshot of me, 'Cor Miss is well FIT.' It might not sound like a lot, but I felt objectified.

Fiona

I once had a boy tell me he was going to 'go full Andrew Tate' on me. When I asked what he meant, he said, 'You know. Violate you.'

Margritte

One boy threw a condom at me – I had my hand on a table and it landed across it. When the condom incident happened I called for SLT support. The Head came but later told me I had wasted his time and should have turned it into a joke.

Abebi

In my first year as a teacher, I had repeated comments about my appearance, which were reported but no sanctions were given apart from detentions set by me. A boy asked me if I sucked sausages and finally threw a pair of girl's knickers across the room! I was told by management that they wouldn't sanction as it could 'blow-up'.

Danielle

On 3 December 2024, Education Secretary Bridget Phillipson wrote an article for *Glamour* magazine,[4] in which she acknowledged the 'insidious hatred' of misogyny in schools. Phillipson acknowledged the fact that this misogyny manifests itself in sexual abuse against teachers, citing the story of one teacher who had told her that a boy had pushed his crotch up against her back in an effort to intimidate her. Phillipson's concerns come despite the fact that there is already existing legislation that should prevent the sexual harassment she so strongly warns against in her article: the Worker Protection (Amendment of Equality Act 2010) Act 2023 came into force on 26 October 2024, introducing a significant shift in how employers – including schools – must deal with sexual harassment. For the

Sexual Harassment in Schools and What to Do About It

first time, the law places a proactive duty on employers to *prevent* sexual harassment, and not just simply respond after it happens. This means that schools can no longer rely on box-ticking policies or reactive investigations alone. They are now legally required to take reasonable steps to create a working environment where harassment is less likely to occur in the first place. For education, this matters. It means thinking not only about staff-to-staff conduct but also about harassment directed at staff by students, parents, or visitors. The duty is clear: prevention is no longer optional, but a legal obligation. And yet despite all of this, incidences of child-on-staff sexual harassment and abuse like those above continue to occur, which can surely only suggest that current legislation doesn't go far enough to protect teachers.

On 29 April 2025, I visited parliament to speak to the Women and Equalities Committee on the topic of misogyny in schools. I was unequivocal in my assertion to the committee that there isn't enough school-specific advice designed to protect teachers from student-perpetrated sexual harassment:

> I don't think there's enough being done to protect female members of staff. In *Keeping Children Safe in Education* there's guidance as to what constitutes *child-on-child* sexual harassment, but I can't find any documentation which outlines to members of staff exactly what constitutes *child-on-staff* sexual harassment. In fact, I often think that as teachers we're expected [to put up with sexual harassment] because we're adults ... The amount of female teachers I've spoken to who have been sexually harassed – physically sexually harassed ... And I mean it when I say women have had things put in their bodies by children and then a day later or even an hour later, they're expected to carry on teaching that child ... I really do think that the government needs to put some guidance in place. There's advice from the unions but actually, as far as I can see, no guidance [to protect teachers] and of course it's happening to

male teachers but largely it's happening to female teachers and for some female teachers it's not just every so often: it's lesson to lesson.[5]

At the time of writing, I stand by what I said then: there is no guidance as to exactly what behaviours constitute child-on-staff sexual harassment. Nothing in black and white. No national definition. No official framework outlining what child-on-staff sexual harassment looks like or what to do about it. This leaves us in a dangerous grey area.

I strongly believe that if the absence of any official guidance from government on what constitutes child-on-staff sexual harassment persists, then school leaders and policy-makers need to ensure that they create their own explicit and visible guidance that protects not only students but teachers too.

Sexual Harassment in Schools: What to Do About It?

As we saw in the introduction, statistics from institutions like Ofsted and charities like UK Feminista, and firsthand accounts of victim abuse on websites like *Everyone's Invited* weave a tattered and discoloured tapestry: for many young people, harassment isn't the exception but the norm. If we're serious about changing this, we have to move beyond acknowledging the problem and start putting concrete, workable solutions in place.

1. Be Clear About What Is and What Isn't Acceptable

Schools are not doing a good enough job of making the boundaries explicit. The uncomfortable truth is that many children (and teachers) don't actually know what sexual harassment looks like. No one has ever spelt it out for them. For some, the behaviour they're engaging in, or having directed at them, is brushed off as banter. My belief is simple: if every single person in a school community – teachers, senior leaders, support staff, students, parents – is told in no uncertain terms what the school defines as sexual harassment, we will see less of it. That means clear policy documents, dedicated information evenings, assemblies that name the behaviours, and explicit teaching woven into the curriculum. When everyone knows the line, it becomes much harder to cross it without consequence.

But can we really lay all the blame at the door of schools? In truth, when the national guidance itself is vague and buried in dense documents, it's little wonder the message isn't filtering down to students...

Keeping Children Safe?

Keeping Children Safe in Education is statutory safeguarding guidance for schools and colleges, which is updated every year to reflect changes in law and new concerns around safeguarding young people. It is a lengthy document consisting of 187 pages split into five parts, each of which is further split into clauses, much like you'd expect in a legal document. There are 562 separate clauses in total. Although the guidance is deemed to be statutory, this statutory obligation to read it only applies to 'governing bodies of maintained schools', 'proprietors of independent schools and non-maintained schools', 'management committees of pupil referral units', and 'senior leadership teams'. Although the document doesn't mandate that teachers must read the document, it does state: 'Governing bodies and proprietors *should* [my emphasis] ensure that those staff who work directly with children read at least Part One of this guidance.'

Clause 32 of the guidance, found in Part One, states the following:

> It is essential that **all** [their emphasis] staff understand the importance of challenging inappropriate behaviours between children that are abusive in nature ... Downplaying certain behaviours, for example dismissing sexual harassment as "just banter", "just having a laugh", "part of growing up" or "boys

being boys" can lead to a culture of unacceptable behaviours, an unsafe environment for children and in worst case scenarios a culture that normalises abuse leading to children accepting it as normal and not coming forward to report it.

Clause 33 goes on to explain that child-on-child abuse 'is most likely to include, but may not be limited to': 'sexual harassment, such as sexual comments, remarks, jokes and online sexual harassment, which may be standalone or part of a broader pattern of abuse.'

A footnote attached to the phrase 'sexual harassment' tells the reader that more information on sexual harassment can be found in section 5: you'll remember that this section is not suggested reading for teachers.

As part of my staff sexual harassment training, I present teachers with four scenarios, and I ask them to tell me if the scenario I've presented is a sexual harassment behaviour according to the statutory guidance *Keeping Children Safe in Education*. The four scenarios are:

- A boy draws a picture of a penis in his exercise book
- A child tells another child about a sex scene they've seen in a film the previous night
- A boy pulls another boy's trousers down for a joke
- A boy wolf whistles at a girl as she passes in the playground

Have a go yourself. Which of these do you think are identified as sexual harassment behaviours in *Keeping Children Safe in Education*?

I have done this quiz with hundreds and hundreds of teachers over the years and never have I found a teacher who can correctly identify these as sexual harassment behaviours or not, according to the so-called statutory guidance.

I am not surprised. The information on exactly what constitutes sexual harassment is lost in a lengthy 187-page document of 562 clauses which many busy teachers don't have time to read among all the marking, planning, and actual teaching they have to do. Even when teachers are inclined to read the information available, the specific guidance as to what constitutes sexual harassment is in a section of the document teachers aren't mandated to read.

I believe the government needs to create a much smaller, more accessible, standalone document, four to five pages at most, that is statutory for all adults working in schools to read regardless of job role, which clearly and directly outlines what sexual harassment looks like and what to do when it occurs. I said as much to the Women and Equalities Committee when I visited in April 2025. Of course, we cannot rely on this happening and so, as with the absence of official guidance on exactly what constitutes child-on-staff sexual harassment in schools, I believe schools should produce their own document – small, accessible, and standalone – which outlines very clearly to teachers (and to school leaders, support workers, students, and parents) exactly what child-on-child sexual harassment is. Only this way can we expect teachers and students to police sexual harassment when it occurs.

Sexual Violence: What Is It?

While I think most teachers would be confident in recognising sexual violence – it's usually more clear-cut than the sometimes nebulous territory of sexual harassment – it's still worth taking a moment to define it. For clarity's sake, let's look at sexual violence first, before moving on to the more common, and often more insidious, issue of sexual harassment.

According to *Keeping Children Safe in Education,* sexual violence in schools are acts defined as criminal offences under the Sexual Offences Act 2003. In plain terms, this includes:

- **Rape** – when someone intentionally penetrates another person's vagina, anus, or mouth with their penis without consent, and without reasonably believing that the other person consents.

- **Assault by penetration** – when someone intentionally penetrates another person's vagina or anus with any part of their body or with an object, without consent, and without reasonably believing there is consent.
- **Sexual assault** – when someone intentionally touches another person in a sexual way without consent, and without reasonably believing there is consent. This covers a wide range of behaviours, from unwanted kissing to touching someone's bottom, breasts, or genitals.
- **Causing someone to engage in sexual activity without consent** – when someone intentionally makes another person take part in sexual activity without their consent, and without reasonably believing there is consent. This could include forcing someone to strip, touch themselves sexually, or engage in sexual activity with another person.

Consent is about having both the *freedom* and the *capacity* to choose. It means saying *'yes'* because you genuinely want to and not because you're pressured, manipulated, scared, or unable to make an informed choice.

Key points about consent to remember:

- Consent can be specific – someone might agree to one sexual act but not another (for example, vaginal but not anal sex) or agree only under certain conditions (such as using a condom).
- Consent can be withdrawn at *any* point, even during sexual activity. If it's withdrawn, the activity must stop immediately.
- For penetration – vaginal, anal, or oral – consent means agreeing *by choice* and having both the freedom and capacity to make that choice.
- A child under 13 can never legally consent to any sexual activity.
- The legal age of consent in the UK is 16.
- Sexual intercourse without consent is rape.

Sexual Harassment in Schools and What to Do About It

Consent is not a one-off box to tick – it's an ongoing, active agreement, and without it, the act becomes a criminal offence.

Sexual Harassment: What Is It?

So, what does the official guidance from the Department for Education say about sexual harassment? It's worth looking at it in black and white because if you know the definitions, you're in a far stronger position to act when you see these behaviours in your classroom or corridors. And if you happen to have some influence in your school, whether that's through a leadership role, a safeguarding remit, or simply the respect of your colleagues, you can use that knowledge to push for clarity. Clarity for staff, students, and parents. Because when everyone is speaking the same language about what sexual harassment is, it becomes a lot harder for it to hide in plain sight.

Sexual harassment means *unwanted conduct of a sexual nature*. It can happen online or offline, inside or outside school. In this context, we're talking specifically about child-on-child sexual harassment.

Sexual harassment is behaviour that is likely to:

- Violate someone's dignity
- Make them feel intimidated, degraded, or humiliated
- Create a hostile, offensive, or sexualised environment

In section 5 of *Keeping Children Safe in Education*, the following are defined as sexual harassment:

- **Sexual comments** – telling sexual stories, making lewd remarks, commenting on clothes or appearance in a sexual way, or calling someone sexualised names.
- **Sexual 'jokes' or taunting** – humour or teasing of a sexual nature, even when framed as 'banter'.
- **Physical behaviour** – deliberately brushing against someone, interfering with their clothes, or any contact that may cross into

sexual violence. The victim's experience and perception must always be considered.
- **Displaying sexual images** – showing pictures, photos, or drawings of a sexual nature.
- **Upskirting** – taking photos or videos under someone's clothing without their permission (a criminal offence).
- **Online sexual harassment** – which may happen on its own or as part of a wider pattern of sexual harassment or sexual violence. This can include:
  o Sharing nude or semi-nude images or videos, whether consensual or not (taking or sharing such images of anyone under 18 is a criminal offence)
  o Sharing unwanted explicit content
  o Sexualised online bullying
  o Unwanted sexual comments or messages, including on social media
  o Sexual exploitation, coercion, or threats
  o Pressuring or coercing others into sharing sexual images or performing sexual acts online.

It's a shame that this information is buried in section 5 of *Keeping Children Safe in Education* – a section that teachers aren't even required to read. The reality is that the onus falls squarely on school leadership teams to make sure staff see it, understand it, and use it. And while the guidance is more detailed than simply throwing around the term 'sexual harassment', it still leaves too much open to interpretation. What exactly constitutes a 'sexual drawing'? Does a scribbled penis on a toilet wall count? What about a 'sexual joke'? Without specifics, we leave staff to decide for themselves and that means inconsistency. There are also glaring omissions: why is wolf-whistling not mentioned? Or sexual staring that leaves someone feeling uncomfortable?

Schools need to take the framework from *Keeping Children Safe in Education* and make it as concrete and relevant to their own setting as possible. Then they need to make that definition visible:

train staff and give them documentation they must be able to prove they've read; talk to students in assemblies about exactly which behaviours will not be tolerated; and make sure parents know too, whether through letters or emails that require confirmation, or through dedicated information evenings. If everyone in the school community knows what counts as sexual harassment, we not only take away the excuses, and the dangerous grey areas where harm can hide, but we also empower victims and bystanders with the knowledge they need to report sexual harassment when it happens.

Protecting the School, Not the Students

Of course, even when individual leaders try to do the right thing, they can find themselves blocked by those above them. I've spoken to staff who've worked tirelessly to create clear, robust sexual harassment policies, only to have them shut down by senior decision-makers worried about 'how it will look'. The fear is that acknowledging the problem will somehow damage the school's reputation, when failing to address it does far greater harm. The following case study, from Claire Jones (name has been changed), a headteacher who experienced exactly this, shows just how deep that resistance can run.

CASE STUDY: BARRIERS TO POLICY, *WRITTEN BY CLAIRE JONES, 2025*

Without a doubt, the number of child-on-child and child-on-adult cases of harassment and abuse has risen significantly in schools. I know this from being a headteacher in my own school but also anecdotally from many other colleagues serving all types of communities up and down the country.

Without a doubt, it is clear that these behaviours from and towards young people are increasing. Recently, an infant school headteacher reached out to me as she was having difficulties getting some parents to understand that their sons touching the girls in their class without consent was not 'boys just being boys' – she wanted help.

Having a Sexual Harassment and Abuse Policy is now an essential for schools. *Keeping Children Safe in Education* provides statutory guidance about 'how schools and colleges should respond to all signs, reports and concerns of child-on-child sexual violence and sexual harassment, including those that have happened outside of the school or college premises, and/or online'.

I no longer wanted to rely on my existing policies: Anti-Bullying Policy, Behaviour Policy, Equality Statement and Objectives were no longer explicit enough about the definitions of sexual violence, sexual harassment, and sexual abuse to be consistently applied. And because of this, instances were not always responded to appropriately, especially if staff got into a battle of semantics with students or parents.

I mean: the Year 10 boy who told his ECT science teacher that he loved her when they were working in a room alone together; the Year 8 boy who chased girls to pinch their bums and boobs, but was never taken too seriously as he was 'harmless' and a Looked After Child; the boy–girl seating arrangement that put vulnerable girls sitting next to over-sexualised boys at the back of class; and the parent that told the receptionist he'd like to rape her.

Each time, I had to pick these instances up after a member of staff had attempted to address the issue but not had the tools to be really explicit: this is sexual violence, harassment, or abuse, and we need to make the victims feel safe AND prevent such instances happening again.

So I set about writing a policy where each of the following was bluntly covered:

- Legal definition of sexual violence
- Legal definition of sexual harassment
- Our commitment to addressing these things
- How we will embed the policy into children's learning, in an age-appropriate way
- How we would respond to reports of sexual violence and harassment (immediately and longer term)
- The actions we would take after a report of sexual violence and harassment
- How we would safeguard other children
- How we would work with parents and carers

However, when you work within a large multi-academy trust, a headteacher cannot always choose to add an extra, potentially controversial policy to the books without some consultation with the central team. And the central team said no. Their reasoning was that the other existing policies should cover these things, but I also feel that they were nervous of drawing the community's attention to such things; if we have a policy then it must mean we have a serious problem, yes?

I think a lot of heads remember the conflict at Anderton Park primary school when their *No Outsiders* curriculum was misunderstood by the community; misinformation deliberately spread and a campaign of protests got so out of hand that headteacher Sarah Hewitt-Clarkson had to get a court injunction to make it stop.

There are plenty of haters out there actively looking to cause trouble, meaning that a policy like this might be seen as poking that nest of vipers; but I continue to think it is essential, and I have not yet given up on it.

2. Teach Students How to Respond to Sexual Harassment

Once students know what sexual harassment is, they're in a far stronger position to respond to it. Right to Be is a non-profit organisation dedicated to ending harassment in all its forms, best known for its '5Ds of Bystander Intervention' – a practical toolkit for safely calling out or disrupting harassment. Their model gives people practical, realistic options for stepping in when they witness harassment, so they're not left thinking, 'I wanted to help, but I didn't know what to do.' For convenience, I've written the explanations of each part of the model as I would explain and deliver them to students.

5Ds Model of Bystander Intervention

i. **DISTRACTION**

Distraction is all about throwing the harassment off course without directly confronting the person doing it. Think of it as hitting the pause button on the situation: creating a moment that gives the person being targeted a chance to breathe, move away, or feel supported.

The key here is simple:
1. Ignore the harasser completely. Focus your attention on the person being harassed.
2. Don't mention the harassment at all. Instead, talk about something totally unrelated.

This can be as subtle or as creative as you like. You might pretend to be lost and ask for directions. You could ask for the time, or act like you've just bumped into an old friend and start chatting about something random. You could simply position yourself physically between the harasser and the target. Or you could 'accidentally' spill your drink, drop your bag, or cause a small commotion that pulls focus away from what's happening.

The beauty of Distraction is that it doesn't announce itself as intervention. No one has to know that's what you're doing, which makes it perfect if you're shy, or if you think confronting the harasser directly might make things worse. Done well, it's subtle, safe, and surprisingly powerful.

ii. **DELEGATION**

Delegation is about bringing in a third party to help you intervene. It's not about passing the buck, or 'wimping out'. It's about recognising that sometimes someone else is better placed, or better equipped, to step in.

The key points are:
1. Find someone nearby who looks ready and willing to help. Often the best person is the one standing right next to you.
2. Ideally, this person should be an adult.
3. Be clear about what you've seen and what you'd like them to do.

This means finding someone in authority. In public it might be a shop owner, a bus driver, or a police officer. In school it might mean a teacher or support worker. It's about asking them to step in. That might mean saying: *'I think that those Year 11 boys are making that Year 10 girl uncomfortable. Can you go over?'*

One thing I've learned from working with young people is that they're often reluctant to do this. They worry about being seen as a 'grass', a 'snake', or a 'snitch'. But you have to make a choice here. You have to decide what kind of person you want to be: someone who fights against injustice or someone who's complicit in it?

Interestingly, when it comes to police involvement, Right to Be advise caution: never call the police unless the person being harassed explicitly asks you to. For some people, such as those from communities with a history of mistrust or harm linked to law enforcement, police involvement can make the situation less safe, not more.

iii. **DOCUMENTATION**

Documentation means recording or taking notes about an incident of harassment. Done well, it can be a powerful way to support the person who's been targeted, but it must be handled with care.

The first step is to assess the situation. Is anyone already helping the person being harassed? If not, your priority isn't to get your phone out but to intervene in another way. Recording without first making sure they're safe can add to their trauma. If someone else is already helping, and you feel it's safe for you to do so, then you can begin documenting what's happening.

I would always warn young people against the use of phones to video record harassment. It can aggravate the situation or put yourself in danger. But, what's to stop you writing down what you hear on your phone as you hear it? It might be that you hear someone in class making some sexist comments or telling a sexual story. Write it down, if you can, so you can use it as evidence. The caution against video recording is important for another reason: often, people who record videos of harassment post the videos online. Never do this: harassment is already a deeply disempowering experience and putting footage of it online without victim consent can strip away even more control from the person who was harmed. It can also make them visible in ways they may not want, and if the footage involves anything illegal, it could drag them into a legal process they're not ready or willing to face.

iv. **DELAY**

Delay is about what you can do after the moment has passed. Not every incident of harassment gives you the chance to step in there and then; sometimes it happens too quickly, or the situation doesn't feel safe to interrupt. But that doesn't mean you do nothing. Checking in with someone afterwards can make a real difference to how they process what happened.

It can be as simple as asking the victim if they're okay and letting them know you saw what happened and that it wasn't okay. You might ask if there's any way you can support them, offer to walk with them to their next destination, or just sit with them for a while. You could share resources or offer to help them make a report if they want to. And if you've documented the incident, you can ask whether they'd like a copy.

Delay isn't about rewinding time. It's about showing the person who was targeted that they weren't invisible, and that someone cared enough to notice and follow up.

I've had students tell me they've been victims of child-on-child sexual harassment and that, in the moment it occurred, they just laughed along nervously or simply froze. Later, they've come to me feeling ashamed that they didn't push back, shout, or report it straight away. Often these students are girls who are known in school for being strong, assertive, and outspoken. But harassment can be shocking, even traumatic, and when you are the victim of sexual harassment it's entirely natural to freeze or to mask discomfort with a laugh. That reaction doesn't make you weak. Nor does it mean you've lost your right to speak up. You can report harassment the next day, the next week, the next month, even years later. The moment might have passed, but your right to be heard hasn't.

v. **DIRECT**

Direct intervention is when you respond to harassment in the moment by naming the behaviour and telling the person to stop. It's the most obvious approach, but it's also the one that carries the most risk. The harasser might turn on you, or the situation might escalate.

Before you jump in, ask yourself four quick questions. The first question is:

1. Am I physically safe?

I know that some of you will probably dismiss this question and think, *'Yeah, I'd get involved no matter what.'* I get that. A lot of you have grown up with the idea that if you step in and save the day, you become the hero, the Disney prince who rescues someone and gets all the adoration and accolades. But the truth is, your desire to be the hero doesn't trump the

victim's right to safety. That's why the next question is just as important or maybe even more so than the first:
2. Is the person being harassed physically safe?
3. Does it seem unlikely that the situation will escalate?
4. Does the person being harassed seem like they want someone to speak up?

If the answer to just one of these questions is 'no', then you need to resort to one of the other 5D methods of intervention. However, if the answer to all four of these questions is 'yes', then you might choose to respond directly. The key is to keep it short and to the point. Don't get drawn into an argument: that's where things spiral. Say your piece, then put your focus back on supporting the person who was targeted.

Direct responses can be as simple as:
- 'That's inappropriate.'
- 'That's harassment.'
- 'Leave them alone.'
- 'Please stop right now.'
- 'They've asked you to leave them alone and I'm here to support them.'

And always remember: your safety matters too. The goal is to help without putting yourself or anyone else in danger.

The 5Ds Model of Bystander Intervention: A Note for Teachers

While the 5Ds Model can be a powerful framework, there are two important caveats I want to be absolutely clear on. The *Distract* and *Direct* methods carry a degree of risk, and for that reason I would only ever discuss them with older students and, even then, only on the understanding that these strategies are for adulthood, not before. My own personal belief is that unless a student is over the age of 18, these two methods should be completely avoided. Safety must come first.

Sexual Harassment in Schools and What to Do About It

If you are teaching the 5Ds Model in a school setting, it may be more appropriate to leave *Distract* and *Direct* out entirely and instead focus on a 3Ds Model of Intervention: *Delay, Document,* and *Delegate.* These are safer, more age-appropriate strategies that still give students meaningful tools to support someone experiencing harassment without putting themselves or anyone else in danger.

The 'Come Off It' Method

In the fight against misogyny in schools, it's not just about what happens when sexual harassment occurs; it's also about the day-to-day culture between students. Not all misogyny is sexual harassment. Sometimes it's a throwaway comment, a crude joke about pornography, or a sexual remark about a girl as she walks past. The problem is, it takes a very strong 15-year-old boy to call out his friends in that moment. Imagine a group of boys in the playground, a female teacher – one they all find attractive – walks past, and one of the boys makes a sexual remark about her. Everyone laughs along. To be the one who steps in and says, *'Actually, that's not okay'* takes a kind of social courage that not many boys, especially teenage boys performing masculinity for an audience, feel they have. The truth is that sexual comments, sexist jokes, and crude conversations about women are often used as bonding tools between boys, so we have to think about how boys can hold each other to account in ways that don't a) invite aggression and defensiveness and/or b) cost them their social standing.

One of the simplest, most effective tools I've found for getting boys to hold each other to account is something I call the *Come Off It* method. When I visit schools, I explain it to boys and girls like this: if someone in your friendship group says something inappropriate – perhaps they objectify a woman, make a homophobic joke, or share something they shouldn't online – you can all make a pledge to call each other in by using the words *'Come off it'* or, even better, *'Come off it, mate.'* That one small phrase does a lot of work. First, it avoids accusatory pronouns like 'you' or 'your', which might make someone feel targeted and, as a result, defensive, aggressive, or both. Second, if you add a term of endearment such as 'mate', 'pal', or an affectionate nickname, you're sending a clear message: *I'm saying this because you're my mate. I care about you. I want you to be a good man, and I'm looking out for you.*

When I talk about the *Come Off It* method in schools, I get friendship groups to pledge to use the phrase next time someone crosses the line and, just as importantly, to accept it with grace if it's said to them. That means resisting the urge to get defensive, taking a second to reflect, and maybe even thanking who called them in. I've revisited schools months and years later and had kids shout it at me across the playground: 'There's the *Come off it, mate* guy!' That tells me it sticks. Teaching young people a safe, non-confrontational way to challenge their friends and showing them how to both give and receive that challenge is powerful. It makes accountability part of the friendship, not a threat to it.

3. Scripted Responses

'Ugh! Romeo's a paedophile.'

It's the same every year. We're a few lessons into *Romeo and Juliet* and we've just read the part in which Juliet's father, Lord Capulet, tells his daughter's eager suitor, Paris, that despite Paris's enthusiasm to marry, he cannot do so until she is older:

> My child is yet a stranger in the world
> She hath not seen the change of fourteen years
> Let two more summers wither in their pride
> Ere we may think her ripe to be a bride.

Sexual Harassment in Schools and What to Do About It

When the more astute children realise that Capulet is telling Paris that his daughter is only 13 years old, what follows is instant and inevitable: groans, laughter, theatrical gagging noises and cries of disgust, and the usual chorus of catcalls about how Romeo needs to be put on some sort of sexual offenders register. Every year, the same reaction and every year, I find myself hovering awkwardly at the front of the room, not quite sure how to respond to the paedophilia jokes causing chaos as they bounce around the classroom. A part of me wants to put this response down to teenage awkwardness or fear disguised as humour. But another part of me knows that this is a teachable moment. An opportunity to teach children that paedophilia jokes are not funny and not appropriate.

I'm not the only English teacher who runs into this problem when teaching *Romeo and Juliet*. When I visit schools to talk about the power of scripted responses, I always ask the English teachers the same question: 'Put your hand up if you've ever had students laugh or joke that Romeo's a paedophile when they find out Juliet is 13.' Without fail, every hand goes up. Then I ask: 'Does it happen every year?' Again, every hand. But what's more telling is the response to my final question. When I ask, 'Have you ever sat down with your department and worked out exactly what to say in response to that moment?', the room falls quiet.

Paedophile jokes in schools are quite common. As are jokes about Jimmy Saville and rape. Sometimes kids just use the word 'rape' inappropriately. They'll use it to mean 'trounce' or 'defeat severely'. For example, 'Tottenham are going to rape Arsenal at the weekend.' Schools are places where students use inappropriate language all the time, but often teachers are at a loss as to how to respond. This is where scripted responses come in.

A scripted response is just that: a short, pre-written script that teachers can use when faced with inappropriate or sexually charged language in the classroom. It might come in the form of a flash card, a laminated prompt, or within a guidance document. The idea is simple: when a student says something like *'I got raped on FIFA last night'* or uses the word 'gay' to insult someone's haircut, and a teacher isn't sure how to respond in the moment, they have something ready. Something that's been thought through. The script is designed to do two things: explain to the student why the language is inappropriate and offer clarification or space for questions. In *BDT?* I wrote about a teacher named James Whale (name has been changed) who created a brilliant script in response to hearing the word 'rape' used inappropriately in his classroom. Whale's script ran as follows:

> Rape is when a man puts his penis into a person's vagina, anus, or mouth without consent. Rape can ruin lives and have serious, lifelong effects on the victim. Using the word casually, as you are doing, is insensitive and inappropriate. Do you understand that? Do you have any questions? Do you want me to explain further?

This script is clear, without flourish, and educational. It reminds students that language matters.

At a school visit recently, I spoke to a teacher who ran an LGBTQ+ group at his school. Students in the group expressed their frustration at the fact that other students in the school were using the word 'gay' as an insult. *'Your haircut's gay.' 'Crying's gay.' 'Those trainers look gay.'* The word was being flung around casually but always with the same message underneath: that being gay is something to mock or avoid. What bothered these students most wasn't just the language but the silence that followed. Often teachers heard the word being used pejoratively but said nothing. So, the students did something about it. They wrote out a simple, firm response that staff could use in the moment. They printed a copy of this script out and it was given to each teacher to use as guide to help them respond to incidents of the word being used inappropriately. This not only helped staff but gave students a signal that someone had their back.

Scripted responses can be a powerful tool for dealing with inappropriate language, especially when the same words or phrases crop up again and again. I do understand that not all teachers are in a position to create a script that can be rolled out on a wider scale. Maybe the Senior Leadership Team aren't comfortable with it. Maybe people are nervous about putting something so direct into writing, worried it'll attract the wrong kind of attention. Fine. But if you're not going to use a script, then at the very least take the time to anticipate when these moments might arise. Think about your subject. Think about your curriculum. When might controversial or misogynistic content crop up? A PSHE lesson on consent? An RSE discussion of Adam and Eve and the fall of man being blamed on Eve? You probably already know when it's likely to happen because it happens every year. And if it's not in your classroom, it might be in the corridors or on the playground. But what you can do is either script a response yourself or sit down with colleagues and agree on one together; it doesn't have to be as formal as a script, but some sort of verbal consensus that provides clarity and education will go a long way.

Towards the end of this chapter you will find a table of scripted responses that you can use in response to incidents of sexual harassment in school.

4. *Educate Students*

We're about to look at a case study that takes a whole-school approach to tackling misogyny: it's an excellent example of the kind of steps any school could take to combat misogyny and sexual harassment. Research is clear: programmes that combine curriculum work with policy, staff training, student involvement, and visible action across the whole school are the ones most likely to shift attitudes and change behaviour.[6] Before we get into that case study, I want to share with you an assembly that can act as the starting point for student education on misogyny within a whole-school strategy. An assembly like this doesn't solve the problem on its own, but it can plant the seed and signal to students that their school is serious about this work.

ASSEMBLY: TACKLING MISOGYNY IN SCHOOLS

Audience: KS3–KS5 (content can be adapted depending on age)

Length: 30–40 minutes

Aim: To help students understand what misogyny is, why it exists, the harm it causes, and how they can safely challenge it.

1. Defining Misogyny (5 minutes)

Younger students:

'Misogyny means a dislike of, or a lack of respect for, women.'

Older students:

'Misogyny means a dislike of, or a lack of respect for, women, but it can also be a fear of, distrust of, or resentment towards women and it's not always loud or obvious. Sometimes it's subtle.'

You might want to explain that misogyny isn't always about individual hatred; it can be embedded in culture, habits, jokes, and expectations.

2. Why Misogyny Exists (10 minutes)

Explain to students that misogyny doesn't appear from nowhere. Instead, it's shaped by multiple forces. Here's a breakdown you can use:

1. **Cultural and historical norms.** For centuries, many societies positioned men as leaders and decision-makers, and women as caregivers. These ideas can still influence attitudes today.
2. **Socialisation and gender roles.** From childhood, boys and girls often receive different messages about how they should behave, what jobs they should do, and what emotions they should show.
3. **Power and dominance dynamics.** In some relationships, workplaces, or institutions, men hold more power. This imbalance can fuel attitudes of entitlement or control over women.
4. **Psychological factors.** Negative personal experiences such as being dumped, insecurities, or fear of vulnerability and rejection can sometimes turn into resentment towards women.
5. **Reinforcement through peer groups and media.** If friends, influencers, or celebrities make sexist jokes or normalise disrespect, it can make misogyny seem acceptable.
6. **Lack of exposure to counter-narratives.** If people never see healthy, respectful relationships between men and women, they might only know harmful stereotypes.
7. **The influence of the Manosphere and toxic male influencers.** Online spaces and figures like Andrew Tate can promote harmful ideas about masculinity, relationships, and gender roles.

3. The Injustices in Society (5–7 minutes)

Share key statistics from UK Feminista:

- Over **a third** of girls have been sexually harassed in school.
- Nearly **one in four** have been **physically** sexually harassed.

Make it clear that misogyny isn't just bad for girls – it's bad for boys too:

- It teaches boys to suppress emotions, damages friendships, and isolates them.
- Misogynists often end up lonely, unhappy, and mistrustful.

4. Unacceptable Behaviours (DfE Guidance) (5 minutes)

Go through the sexual harassment behaviours outlined by the Department for Education. These might include:

- Sexual comments and jokes
- Sexualised name-calling
- Physical contact without consent
- Displaying sexual images
- Upskirting (illegal)
- Online harassment (sharing nudes without consent, sexualised bullying, unwanted sexual comments/messages)

Stress that these behaviours are never 'banter', but they are harmful and unacceptable.

5. The 5Ds Model of Bystander Intervention (7–8 minutes)

Teach students the five ways they can respond when they witness harassment:

1. **Distract:** Interrupt the situation indirectly.
2. **Delegate:** Get help from someone else.
3. **Document:** Record what's happening (with care and consent).
4. **Delay:** Check in with the person afterwards, or report harassment after it's happened, however much time has passed.
5. **Direct:** Confront the behaviour (older students/adults only).

Explain your caveat: Distract and Direct carry more risk and should not be used by anyone under 18. In schools, focus on Delay, Document, and Delegate.

6. The Come Off It Method (5 minutes)

Explain this as a safe, non-confrontational way to call out inappropriate language within a friendship group:

- Say *'Come off it'* or *'Come off it, mate'* (adding a term of endearment softens it and shows care).
- Avoid 'you' or 'your' – this reduces defensiveness.
- Make a pledge as a group to use it when someone crosses the line.
- If someone says it to you, reflect instead of reacting aggressively. Maybe even thank them.

5. Adopt a Whole-School Approach to Tackling Misogyny

What does a whole-school approach to tackling misogyny look like in practice? Too often, schools hear the phrase 'whole-school approach' and think it means an extra policy or a one-off training session. The research is clear: sustained change happens when the message is reinforced at every level: policy, environment, staff culture, student voice, and parental engagement. The following case study is a brilliant example of this in action. It shows a school refusing to treat sexualised comments as harmless 'banter' and instead committing to a long-term cultural shift, where every member of the community understands their role in challenging misogyny.

> **CASE STUDY: A WHOLE-SCHOOL APPROACH TO TACKLING MISOGYNY, *WRITTEN BY MATTHEW COOPER*, DEPUTY HEAD AT ENLUTC**
>
> As a school, we recognised that one of our most pressing cultural issues was the frequency of comments made by boys towards girls that were sexualised in nature. We also noticed that these remarks were often dismissed by students, and occasionally staff, as mere 'banter'. This culture of minimisation was allowing harmful attitudes to go unchallenged and was eroding the sense of safety and respect we want all students to feel, particularly our female students.
>
> In response, we undertook a whole-school approach to tackle this issue head-on.
>
> We began with staff training. A dedicated CPD session focused specifically on sexual harassment in schools, equipping staff with not only the knowledge but the language to challenge it.

We developed and distributed scripted responses to common transgressions [see below] that staff could use in the moment, which many said gave them a new level of confidence in addressing this behaviour consistently.

To reinforce that this was not just a school issue but a community-wide one, we emailed parents to explain our stance. In this communication, we made it clear that staff would be using precise language such as 'sexual harassment' and 'misogyny' when reporting incidents, and that these terms may now appear in behaviour reports when appropriate. This transparency helped build a sense of shared responsibility between school and home.

We also looked at how our environment could play a part in shifting culture. We introduced a series of posters across the school that directly challenged the notion that sexual harassment is 'just banter' or 'harmless flirting'. Alongside these, we displayed posters featuring quotes from positive male role models who spoke about leadership, accountability, and respect. The idea was to offer alternative narratives of masculinity that weren't rooted in dominance or bravado.

A central part of our approach was a one-hour assembly delivered to each year group individually. This wasn't a lecture; it was a guided conversation covering sexual harassment, misogyny, and dominance-based masculinity. We worked hard to reframe masculinity in a positive light, anchored in kindness, responsibility, and courage.

As part of preparing the assembly, we involved a student focus group. One of the most powerful outcomes from that group was the development of a phrase: 'We're better than that.' This became a core part of our messaging, something students could say to challenge inappropriate comments without escalating tension. You'll see this phrase across our posters and featured in the assembly itself. It came from the students, and that gives it real strength.

Since the assembly, the phrase 'We're better than that' has really stuck with both students and staff. Yes, some students now use it in a subversive, almost tongue-in-cheek way, but I don't see that as a problem. In fact, I'd argue it's part of its strength. They still know exactly when and how to use it, and it gives them a way to call out poor behaviour without it feeling like a formal telling-off. It's more of a knowing nudge: *'I'm saying this as a joke, but we both know what you've just said isn't okay.'* Delivered in that tone, it's usually taken in good humour, but crucially, it still brings the conversation to a halt.

We also wanted to provide students with accessible and safe ways to report concerns. From our surveys and focus group feedback, it became clear that students wanted some form of anonymous reporting. While true anonymity isn't possible in a safeguarding context, we launched two new email addresses to bridge that gap. These provide students with a way to report concerns without face-to-face confrontation – something many told us would make them more likely to speak up.

Finally, we wanted to prepare our students for the world beyond school. We recorded an interview with a company director who discussed how the issues of misogyny and sexual harassment manifest in the workplace, and the real-world consequences of inappropriate behaviour. Hearing it from someone in industry helped make the message land by showing students that the expectations we're setting here aren't just about school rules; they're about life.

Sexual Harassment in Schools and What to Do About It

> All of these measures form part of a cultural shift we are committed to sustaining. This isn't a tick-box exercise but a long-term commitment to creating a school culture where everyone feels safe, respected, and empowered to challenge unacceptable behaviour.

Case Study Reflection

What stands out most about this case study is its refusal to treat misogyny as an add-on issue. Too many schools respond to sexualised language or harassment with a reactive approach without ever addressing the culture that allows those behaviours to flourish. Here, the school has recognised that the problem isn't just the comments themselves but the normalisation of those comments through the 'it's just banter' defence. That's an important distinction. When harmful language is minimised by staff, it sends a signal to students that the boundaries are negotiable. When it's minimised by peers, it strengthens the peer-group norms that keep it going.

The decision to start with staff training is exactly the right one. You can't expect consistent challenge from staff if they're not confident in what to say or if they fear their response will be questioned. Those scripted responses are really powerful: they take the hesitation out of the moment and replace it with a clear, practised response. It's the difference between silence and action. With Matthew's permission I've included them below for you to use in your setting.

Bringing parents into the conversation is another strong move. Too often, families hear about incidents only when a sanction is given, which can make the school seem punitive rather than proactive. By stating up front that terms like 'misogyny' and 'sexual harassment' will be used in behaviour reports, the school has set expectations and invited parents into the shared responsibility of culture change.

Unmasking the Manosphere

Visible environmental changes – such as posters which challenge 'banter', highlight positive male role models and include student-created slogans such as 'We're better than that' – turn abstract values into daily reminders. They make it harder for harmful attitudes to hide in plain sight. Crucially, in this case, the fact that slogan came from the students themselves gives it a credibility that top-down messaging often lacks.

The anonymous reporting system shows that the school has listened to students' concerns about speaking up. It also bridges a common gap: wanting to challenge behaviour but not feeling safe or confident enough to do it publicly.

Finally, linking the conversation to life beyond school through the workplace interview reframes the issue as preparation for adulthood, not just another rule to follow in uniform. That's a message that sticks.

This isn't tokenistic. It's sustained, layered, and culturally aware. It's the kind of approach that, over time, changes not just behaviour but beliefs.

Table of Scripted Responses		
Student Behaviour	**Scripted Response**	**Expanded Scripted Response (Explicitly Framing as Sexual Harassment)**
Sexualised name-calling (e.g. 'slut', 'whore, 'player')	'That language is unacceptable. We treat each other with respect here. This is an example of sexual harassment.'	'Calling someone a "slut" or similar names is a form of sexual harassment. It creates a culture where people – especially girls – are judged unfairly based on gender or perceived behaviour. We do not tolerate that here.'

Sexual Harassment in Schools and What to Do About It

Unwanted touching (e.g. bra strap pulling, poking, brushing against)	'Touching someone without their consent is sexual harassment. It is not acceptable, and it stops now.'	'This behaviour is sexual harassment because it violates someone's personal space and can make them feel uncomfortable or unsafe. Everyone has the right to feel secure in this environment.'
Sexually explicit jokes or comments	'That joke is inappropriate and is a form of sexual harassment. We do not joke about things that make others feel uncomfortable or unsafe.'	'Sexual jokes, especially those about assault or consent, contribute to a culture where sexual harassment is normalised. We expect everyone to uphold respect and challenge harmful behaviour.'
Spreading sexual rumours	'Spreading rumours about someone's personal life is sexual harassment. It can be damaging and is not tolerated here.'	'Sexual rumours can seriously impact someone's mental wellbeing and reputation. This is sexual harassment, and we must be mindful of the impact our words have on others.'
Sharing inappropriate images or pressuring someone for nudes	'This is serious – pressuring or sharing explicit images is sexual harassment and illegal. I need to report this.'	'Sharing or requesting explicit images without consent is not just inappropriate – it's a crime. This is a serious form of sexual harassment that can have legal consequences. If this has happened to you or someone you know, please speak to a trusted adult immediately.'

Dismissing complaints as 'banter'	'Calling something "banter" does not excuse sexual harassment. If it makes someone feel uncomfortable, it's not okay.'	'Minimising harmful behaviour as "banter" allows sexual harassment to continue unchecked. We all have a responsibility to ensure that our words and actions promote respect, not harm.'
Justifying behaviour with 'That's just how boys/girls are'	'Saying "that's just how boys/girls are" dismisses sexual harassment. Everyone is responsible for their own behaviour.'	'Stereotypes like this enable a culture of harassment and disrespect. Sexual harassment is never acceptable, and we must hold ourselves to higher standards of respect and accountability.'
Discussing pornography	'Bringing up pornography in school is inappropriate and can contribute to sexual harassment. Let's focus on respectful conversations.'	'Talking about pornography in a school setting can make others uncomfortable and reinforce unrealistic or harmful ideas about relationships. Discussions like this can contribute to sexual harassment by normalising objectification.'
Discussing OnlyFans models	'This conversation is inappropriate for school and contributes to sexual harassment by objectifying people. Let's shift the discussion.'	'When we talk about people only in terms of their appearance or profession in this way, it reduces them to objects. That contributes to a culture where sexual harassment is normalised, and we need to be better than that.'

Discussing their sexual exploits	'Talking about your sex life in school is inappropriate and can constitute sexual harassment. We respect each other's privacy.'	'Discussing sexual experiences in a public setting can make others uncomfortable and pressures people into conversations they may not want to have. This is a form of sexual harassment because it disregards the comfort and consent of others in the conversation.'
Making comments about how attractive or unattractive someone is, even if they are not in the room	'Commenting on someone's appearance in this way is a form of sexual harassment. We do not reduce people to their looks.'	'Even if the person isn't present, making sexual or degrading comments about their appearance contributes to a culture of sexual harassment. Everyone deserves to be treated with dignity and respect, whether they are in the room or not.'

The Final Word

Tackling misogyny in schools isn't about a one-off assembly, or a poster campaign that gets forgotten, or unread lines in a policy document. It's about creating a culture where respect is non-negotiable, where harmful language is challenged every time, and where students feel both safe and responsible for holding each other to account. It's uncomfortable work. It takes persistence, and it will put people in awkward conversations. But it's worth it. Because when we challenge misogyny, we're not just protecting girls; we're also helping boys to grow into kinder, braver, more authentic men. And that's the kind of legacy any school should be proud of.

Notes

1. https://committees.parliament.uk/writtenevidence/67952/html/
2. www.thebodypro.com/article/teens-report-peer-pressure-sex
3. https://estyn.gov.wales/system/files/2021-12/Experiences%20of%20peer-on-peer%20sexual%20harassment%20among%20secondary%20school%20pupils%20in%20Wales_0.pdf
4. www.glamourmagazine.co.uk/article/bridget-phillipson-misogyny-young-boys-education
5. https://parliamentlive.tv/Event/Index/b491296f-c32a-48cd-90fd-ff412ee65cb2
6. Scottish Government. (2020). *Preventing violence against women and girls – what works: Effective investments summary*. Scottish Government. www.gov.scot/publications/effective-investments-summary-works-prevent-violence-against-women-girls-policy-practitioners/

# 4 Discussing Misogyny

Why Boys Say Misogynistic Things

When I first started out speaking and writing about misogyny, my first assumption when a boy expressed a sexist or misogynistic opinion was that he was a monster-raving, sexually deviant, knuckle-dragging, fully paid-up member of the National Union of Misogyny. I'd assume that, at best, he hated women and that, at worst, he was dangerous. That he would grow up and cause harm.

But as I've now come to realise, misogyny in boys isn't always coming from hate. Sometimes it comes from other places: fear, rejection, confusion, a desire to belong. The sooner we start accepting the reasons many boys give voice to misogyny, the sooner we can better start doing something about it.

Misogyny as a Mask

A lot of boys don't genuinely believe the things they say. Not deep down. They say them because they're trying to be funny. Or to fit in. In a recent study from 2024 exploring how boys respond to masculinity workshops,[1] the researchers noted a recurring pattern: when boys expressed misogynistic or homophobic views, it was rarely in isolation. Instead, these comments were delivered with a sideways

Unmasking the Manosphere

glance, a stifled giggle, or a shared moment of eye contact with a mate across the room. The researchers describe the discomfort of witnessing these interactions – not just because of the content of the speech but because of the unspoken choreography that surrounded it. Misogyny, here, wasn't just opinion; it was *performance*. A script for belonging. Those giggles and glances are needed in order to prove that you're one of the lads, even if that means saying things you don't fully believe. The boys weren't necessarily trying to shock the researchers – they were trying to impress each other. And this is the unsettling truth we often overlook: for many boys, misogyny is not born from hatred but from hunger. A hunger to be accepted. To be laughed with, not laughed at. To be seen.

I remember the time a 15-year-old boy once said to me during a workshop on the topic of masculinity something along the lines of *'Girls say they want nice guys but really they love it when you're a bit of a player.'* It would have been easy for me to come down hard on him, tell him off, shame him, or send him out the room. But instead, I asked him where he'd got that idea. Turns out he'd got it off a 'masculinity coach' he'd seen on YouTube, who had told him that to get girls to respect you, you had to be being cold, unavailable, and dominant. If I'm honest, there's a part of my own fragile masculinity that instinctively agrees with the idea that 'nice guys finish last'. But then, the more reflective, more mature adult in me realises there are plenty of horrible blokes who end up with nothing and there are plenty of really nice fellas in really loving relationships. But this boy didn't have that knowledge at just 15 years old. All he had was YouTube.

Misogyny as a Reaction to Rejection

A lot of boys are lonely – even those who don't appear to be so. A lot of the teachers I speak to talk to me about 'groups of boys' and their 'pack mentality'. While I don't agree with the assumptions

Discussing Misogyny

made with comments like this, I do know that, of course, there are boys who are part of large social groups. What I also know is that sometimes, when you're part of a large group of boys, all competing for dominance and attention, it can be very easy to feel extremely lonely.

Also, a lot of boys feel ignored. They don't feel desirable, powerful, or respected. So when some alpha male influencer comes along and tells them that girls are the problem, or that girls only go for hard men, or that nice guys finish last, or that the system is rigged against boys, it's seductive. These boys are no longer losers – they're victims.

This is how misogyny becomes appealing and something that boys readily give voice to. Not because it's evil, but because it offers boys something: an explanation. A sense of control. A way to make sense of pain.

Misogyny as Banter

Misogyny is not always a product of some deep-rooted trauma. Sometimes boys say misogynistic things for one simple reason: to get a laugh.

For many boys, one way of earning respect is through humour, even if that humour is cruel. Making fun of girls, objectifying them, and reducing them to stereotypes gets a reaction. And many boys crave reaction. If everyone laughs when you say something sexist, it feels like you've just won something. You're visible. You're powerful. You're in.

This doesn't mean that we should excuse it. But it does mean we have to understand the social function it serves. Because if we want boys to drop misogynistic banter, we've got to give them something to replace it with – a different way to belong. A better kind of status.

Misogyny as Confusion

A lot of the boys I meet genuinely don't understand what misogyny is. They think it's only about hating women. I remember talking at one school to a group of Year 7 students about combatting misogyny and respecting female boundaries. When the talk had finished and students were being dismissed, a tiny bespectacled boy on the front row pinched the backside of the girl in front of him. I saw it happen. I also saw a teacher at the side of the assembly hall had seen it happen. This same teacher had also seen that I had seen it happen. In a fit of embarrassment, the teacher stomped over to the boy and barked at him: *'Apologise to Matt. Tell him you're a misogynist!'* The boy, who looked as bemused as I nearly was, lip trembling, squeaked his reply: *'I'm not a misogynist. I love women. That's why I touch their bums.'*

I don't think this boy was a misogynist. Do I think his behaviour was misogynistic? Yes, and that's just as bad. Misogyny isn't always a deep-rooted hatred of women. Sometimes it's more casual. It lives in assumptions. It shows up when boys talk over girls, when they rate them out of 10, when lads laugh at a rape joke, or when they act like being emotional makes someone weak. No one had ever helped that boy see the bigger picture – that misogyny isn't always evil attempts to hurt other people. That it can reveal itself in other ways too.

What Boys Need

Boys need the space to be confused. To say the wrong thing and not be crucified for it.

They need people who will sit with them in their mess of frustration, or rejection, or isolation, and help them untangle it rather than shame them into silence. If we want boys to unlearn misogyny, we can't start with accusation. We must start with understanding. And none of this is easy. Especially for women in schools – the teachers,

Discussing Misogyny

mentors, and support staff – who've spent a lifetime on the receiving end of misogyny. For some, the comments boys make aren't just 'banter' or 'boundary pushing'. They echo real experiences of harassment, humiliation, or even trauma. Asking those staff members to respond with curiosity instead of condemnation can feel like asking too much. This is why schools need to approach this work as a collective effort that recognises the emotional labour involved and doesn't leave women alone to carry it. Understanding boys should never come at the cost of protecting women. It's about building a culture where both matter.

What Doesn't Work

When we hear a boy say something offensive or cruel about girls, something in our gut reacts. We feel disgusted. Angry. Protective. We want to do something: stop it, fix it, shut it down. But the things we instinctively do in those moments such as silencing, scolding, or punishing often don't work. Sometimes they even backfire. Here are some pitfall responses to avoid:

1. **The Public Telling-Off**

    I don't blame teachers for telling boys off when they say something sexist. Sometimes it's an instinctive response because we're horrified at what we've heard, or sometimes it's a conscious decision to show him – and the rest of the class – that those sorts of comments are not acceptable. Public discipline has its place. If something is harmful and loud, we need to step in. But if every sexist comment gets handled with public humiliation, all we're doing is teaching boys to hide it better. And the reality is that a public telling-off might not even work: A 2020 study published in the *Journal of Positive Behaviour Interventions* tracked 149 teachers and over 300 students across multiple schools.[2] The researchers looked at whether teacher reprimands actually changed student behaviour over time. The answer? Not really. While telling a student off might shut something down in the moment, it didn't reduce future disruptions – and it didn't improve engagement either. The study makes a strong case: if we want long-term change, we need more than a raised eyebrow and a stern voice

Public tellings-off don't change boys' beliefs. They just change who they express those beliefs around.

2. **The Moral Lecture**

I've done this countless times. I've stopped the class and launched into a pontification on the wrongs of misogyny and patriarchal society. When we do things like this, it's well meaning and heartfelt, but to the boy in question? It's probably just noise. He's already shut down. Rather than listening to you, he's instead thinking about how to avoid being the centre of attention next time. What he needs isn't a speech. It's a conversation. And those rarely happen in front of 30 other people.

3. **Overusing *'That's Inappropriate'***

Teachers say this a lot. It's usually said with good reason, but if it's our only move, it stops being helpful.

While the word 'inappropriate' tells a boy that a line has been crossed, what it doesn't tell him is why. And for many boys, especially those whose worldviews are shaped online, they genuinely don't understand what they've done wrong. They think they're being funny. Or honest. Or just 'saying what everyone's thinking'. If all they hear is 'That's inappropriate', it becomes a code word for 'Don't get caught'.

Instead, we need to build boys' understanding. *What made it inappropriate? Who did it harm? What belief is hiding underneath that comment?* They're the kind of questions we need to be providing answers to.

4. **Avoiding It Altogether**

According to UK Feminista, 27% of teachers would not feel comfortable tackling a sexist incident that they witnessed in school.[3] As teachers, often we hear the joke, or we catch the comment, and we *know* it was wrong. But we freeze. We're not sure what to say. We're worried we'll handle it badly, so we ignore it. Interestingly, 74% of the teachers who said they lacked confidence in tackling sexist incidents in school said that the reason they lacked confidence was because they didn't feel supported by leaders in school.

The problem is, silence has its own volume. It tells the other boys in the room that no one's going to challenge them. It tells the girls that no one's going to protect them. And it tells the boy who said it that maybe he's right.

5. **Making It All About Us**

    Sometimes, in our attempts to challenge misogyny, we make ourselves the centre of the story.

    'I'm offended.'

    'I'm disappointed.'

    'I'm shocked someone in this school would think that.'

Again, this is understandable. But when we respond from a place of personal emotion, we're asking the boy to care about our feelings. And most of the time, he doesn't. Not because he's heartless, but because we haven't earned that emotional connection yet.

The better route is to ask him how he feels. Where he got the idea from. Whether he's ever thought about the impact of what he just said. Shift the focus back to his thinking, not our outrage.

What's the Cost of Getting It Wrong?

If we don't respond at all, or if we respond in ways that shut boys down, we push them further into the Manosphere or further embed their misogynistic beliefs. We confirm what they've already been told: that 'you can't say anything anymore', that 'the system is against boys', that 'feminism hates men'. Once boys have bought into that narrative, it's harder to pull them out.

Unmasking the Manosphere

The goal isn't to win an argument. The goal is to keep them in the conversation.

What Does Work: Empathetic Interventions

As we've seen, you don't fix misogyny by shouting or humiliating it out of a boy. You definitely don't reach a boy's heart by making him feel stupid. To challenge misogyny effectively, we need more than outrage: we need empathy. This doesn't mean having empathy for the viewpoint. It does mean having empathy for the boy who holds it.

Misogyny as Armour

It can be useful, when a boy says something sexist, to ask yourself: What's underneath?

Because often, for a boy, misogyny is a defence mechanism:

- A way to impress his mates
- A way to cope with rejection
- A way to feel powerful when he feels small
- A way to sound grown-up when he feels out of his depth

He might not even believe what he's saying, but if it gets him a laugh, a nod, or a place in the in-crowd, he'll keep saying it. That doesn't make it okay. But it does help us understand how to respond. So now, let's take a look at ten effective ways to engage boys in positive discussions about masculinity.

Ten Tips to Discuss Misogyny Effectively with Boys

1. **Start with Curiosity**
   When a boy voices something problematic, the instinct might be to shut it down fast.

Discussing Misogyny

But pause.

Instead of:
- 'That's sexist.'
- 'You can't say that.'

Try:
- 'That's a strong opinion – where does it come from?'
- 'Tell me more – what makes you say that?'
- 'Who or what has influenced your thinking there?'

Asking these questions doesn't signal agreement. But it does show the boy that you're not there to punish him but to understand him. And if he feels understood, he's far more likely to listen.

Dr Emily Setty, Associate Professor in Criminology at the University of Surrey, is an expert in misogyny amongst young people and author of *Reimagining Relationships and Sex Education: A Safe Uncertainty Approach to Adolescent Intimacies*. She suggests that as well as asking questions of boys, we can encourage them to ask questions of us and of the opinions they hear and the online content they consume: 'Encourage boys to ask questions rather than adopt fixed positions. Curiosity can be a powerful antidote to defensiveness and opens up space for boys to challenge taken-for-granted norms and scripts. Of course, the answers boys receive may lead to feelings of uncertainty. But that's okay too …'

2. **Hold Space for Uncertainty and Ambivalence**

    Dr Setty puts great emphasis on uncertainty as part of the discussion process: 'Rather than seeking immediate clarity or correction, invite boys to explore tensions in how they feel, think and act around gender. Sitting with uncertainty can help develop deeper self-awareness and open up more meaningful, reflective conversations.'

3. **Hold Space for Discomfort**

    Sometimes boys are simply weaponising misogyny. They know that their comments will wind people up. They'll say something outrageous just to provoke a reaction. Even this doesn't always

signify that the boy genuinely believes the opinions he's giving voice to. It's theatre. It's attention seeking. When you sense that a boy is acting out this way, it's okay to let him squirm. Simply let the silence hang and then calmly ask:
- 'Do you want to explore that with me or are you just trying to get a reaction?'
- 'What do you think would happen if you said that in front of a prospective employer?'
- 'What's the cost of saying that sort of thing in public? What might happen to you? How might others respond?'

Empathetic intervention doesn't mean being soft. It means being steady.

4. **Treat Boys' Perspectives as Data, Not Errors**

   Setty went on to tell me, after I'd asked her how best to discuss misogyny with boys, 'Even when perspectives include problematic elements, they can illuminate the social, emotional and cultural conditions boys are navigating. Use them as starting points to understand what's shaping their views, rather than rushing to fix or re-educate.'

5. **Use the 'Sliding Scale'**

   Not all misogyny is the same. While some boys may be knee-deep in red-pill ideology, convinced that they've found 'the truth', other boys might simply be parroting things they don't understand.

   Your approach should match their stage of thinking. This table looks at the 'sliding scale' of misogynistic thinking and outlines the appropriate intervention:

Scale	Characteristics	Appropriate Intervention
Stage 1: Unthinking Repeaters	Say things they've heard online or from (often older) peers. Don't fully understand the implications of what they are saying.	Curiosity, gentle challenge, invite to reflect. *'Sounds like you've picked that up from somewhere. Have you ever questioned it? Why does it resonate?'*

Discussing Misogyny

Stage 2: Chronic Challengers	Push boundaries regularly. Know that what they're doing and saying provokes people.	Calm firmness, name the pattern, ask them to step into someone else's shoes. *'You've made a few comments like this recently. What are you hoping to get out of them?'*
Stage 3: Committed Believers	Deeply engaged in misogynistic ideologies. Often isolating themselves from mainstream school culture.	One-to-one work, long-term relationships, reframing identity and purpose. *'I know you see the world differently. I'm not here to mock that – I'm here to help you think critically about the factors who've shaped those beliefs.'*

6. **Make It About Values, Not Blame**
   Boys will shut down if they think they're being labelled a bad person. So instead of moralising, connect their behaviour to values they already care about:
   o 'You strike me as someone who cares about fairness. Can I show you how that comment might land unfairly?'
   o 'You talk a lot about respect. What would it look like to show that in how we talk about girls?'
   o 'You seem loyal to your male friends. Are you loyal to the women in your life?'
   This isn't about catching them out. It's about calling them in.
7. **Don't Rush the Result**
   The transformation from misogyny to non-misogyny or anti-misogyny doesn't happen immediately. You might not see a magical change in the moment. That's okay. A seed doesn't sprout just because you stared at the soil for five minutes. Sometimes the boy will think about it later, in bed, or when

something similar happens again. Sometimes it'll be weeks. Sometimes he'll come back to you and say, *'You know that thing you said...'* The win isn't always instant. The win is that he stayed in the room. He listened. You gave him the chance to reflect and he took it, even if he didn't show it yet.

8. **When Boys Open Up, Stay with It**

    Occasionally, a boy will surprise you. You'll ask what's going on underneath the misogyny, and he'll actually tell you about heartbreak, rejection, loneliness, or feeling ignored. This is your inroad. Because misogyny often thrives where boys have no other language for pain. When you offer them a new script that says, *you're allowed to feel, and it doesn't make you weak,* you're not just challenging misogyny but replacing it with something better.

9. **Introduce Gender as Relational, Not Adversarial**

    'Move beyond "boys vs girls" framings', suggests Setty, 'and emphasise that gender relations are co-constructed and that empathy, mutual understanding and shared vulnerability can be foundations for better relationships and more authentic identities.'

10. **Work Towards a Shared Vision of Positive Gender Futures**

    According to Setty, it can be useful to 'frame conversations not only in terms of what must be unlearned but what can be built: relationships that are mutual, meaningful, and liberating for all genders. Invite boys into this vision as co-creators, not as problems to be fixed.'

Language to Use – and Avoid

Talking to boys about misogyny can feel like walking a tightrope. Say nothing, and you're complicit. Say the wrong thing, and they shut down. Use too much force, and they push back harder. So, the question becomes: how do we talk to boys in a way that keeps them open, reflective, and willing to change?

A big part of the answer lies in how we speak: not just what we say but the tone we use and create, and the words we use.

The Problem with Shutting It Down

When a boy says something misogynistic, it's easy to reach for blunt language:

- 'That's sexist.'
- 'You can't say that.'
- 'Do you have any idea how offensive that is?'
- 'Don't be disgusting.'

While these reactions are understandable, they also shut the door. They create defensiveness. They tell the boy: you're bad. And once a boy feels judged, he's not thinking about the harm he's caused but about how unfair you're being.

What Works Better: Language That Disarms, Not Defeats

Try this instead:

- 'That's an interesting thing to say. Where did you get that idea?'
- 'Say more about that. I want to understand how you're thinking.'
- 'How do you think that would sound to someone who's experienced sexual harassment?'
- 'Would you be comfortable if someone said that about you?'
- 'What would you say if a girl said the same thing about boys?'

This kind of language slows things down by lowering the emotional temperature. It shows that you're not just here to punish but to explore. It also communicates something vital: I believe you're capable of thinking this through. That's powerful. Because when boys feel respected, they're far more likely to reflect.

A Simple Rule: Say with, Not at

When a boy airs an offensive misogynistic opinion, it's important that we *discuss with* him, rather than *talk at* him. The following table compares the kind of things we might say that immediately shut the conversation down, with questions we might ask to encourage the boy to critically reflect upon his opinions.

Shutting Down	Opening Up
'That's sexist.'	'What makes you say that?'
'You can't say that.'	'Have you ever thought about how that lands?'
'That's disgusting.'	'Can I challenge you on that a bit?'
'You're being misogynistic.'	'Where did you pick that idea up from?'
'Watch your mouth.'	'Let's break that down together.'
'That's not appropriate.'	'I want to help you see another angle.'

Note that the questions in the second column don't let the misogyny slide; they just don't come in swinging. They keep the boy engaged rather than humiliated.

Don't Make It About Being 'Nice to Women'

One trap we often fall into when discussing misogyny with students is making anti-misogyny all about being polite to girls, as if misogyny is just a manners problem. When we say things like *'You should respect women because they're your mum/sister/daughter'* or *'How would you feel if someone said that to your sister/mum/nan'*, we're just framing girls as extensions of men. Comments like these don't ask boys to see girls as full human beings. Instead, they ask boys to protect 'their' girls.

What's better, is language that humanises girls on their own terms:

- 'Do you think girls should feel unsafe walking home?'
- 'How do you think that joke affects girls in this room?'

- 'What would it be like to be on the receiving end of that kind of comment every day?'

Anti-misogyny isn't about politeness. It's about empathy.

The Power of Tone

Language isn't just words: it's also tone. You can say the exact same phrase in two different ways and get two wildly different outcomes.

'You alright?' said with curiosity = invitation.
'You alright?' said with aggression = warning.

With boys, especially boys who are posturing or playing up, your tone can completely change whether they hear you or ignore you. You don't need to act like their mate. But you do need to sound like someone who sees them and not just someone who wants to correct them.

It's Okay to Get It Wrong

You're not going to get it right every time. Sometimes you'll say the wrong thing. Sometimes you'll come in too hot. Sometimes you'll freeze. That's fine. You can always come back to a boy the next day and say, *'I've been thinking about what you said yesterday, and I want to talk about it properly.'* That's not weakness. That's modelling what it means to reflect, rethink, and stay human.

The Final Word

Most boys who say sexist things aren't monsters. They're confused. Curious. Sometimes hurting. And if we only ever punish or shut them down, we miss the chance to reach them. This work of holding boys to account while also holding space for them to reflect and grow is slow, messy, and emotionally demanding. But it's also where the change happens: in the quiet moments when a boy says something awful and an adult says, *'Let's talk about that,'* instead of just walking away.

Notes

1. Milne, B., Cambazoglu, I., Haslop, C., & Ringrose, J. (2024). Researching young masculinities during the rise of 'misogyny influencers': Exploring affective and embodied discomfort and dilemmas of feminist and queer researchers. *YOUNG*, *33*(5), 494–512. https://doi.org/10.1177/11033088241295844
2. Caldarella, P., Larsen, R. A. A., Williams, L., Wills, H. P., & Wehby, J. H. (2020). "Stop doing that!": Effects of teacher reprimands on student disruptive behavior and engagement. *Journal of Positive Behavior Interventions*, *23*(3), 163–173. https://doi.org/10.1177/1098300720935101 (Original work published 2021)
3. UK Feminista & National Education Union. (2017). *It's just everywhere: A study on sexism in schools – and how we tackle it*. National Education Union & UK Feminista.

5

Male Violence Against Women and Girls

Why Male Violence Against Women and Girls?

In this chapter, I refer to *MVAWG* – Male Violence Against Women and Girls – rather than simply *VAWG*, which is the more commonly used term in policy and education spaces.[1] This is a deliberate decision, and one rooted in clarity and accountability.

While *VAWG* highlights the disproportionate levels of violence experienced by women and girls, it's a passive construction. It describes what happens but not who is doing it. By omitting the gender of the perpetrators, *VAWG* can unintentionally obscure a vital truth: most violence against women and girls is perpetrated by men.

That's not just my opinion. It's what the data tells us: consistently, across time, and across countries. Whether we're looking at domestic abuse,[2] sexual harassment, rape,[3] stalking, or image-based abuse, the vast majority of perpetrators are male. Naming that matters. Because if we want to prevent this violence, we have to be honest about where it's coming from.

Using *MVAWG* isn't about vilifying men and boys. Rather, it's about opening the door to more meaningful conversations with boys and young men about power, entitlement, empathy, and responsibility.

Unmasking the Manosphere

If we can't name the problem accurately, we can't equip the next generation to understand or challenge it.

As educators, we often ask our students to speak with clarity. We encourage them to use precise language, to say what they really mean. This is me trying to do the same.

Why MVAWG Belongs in a Book for Teachers

MVAWG might not be something you associate with your classroom, your corridor, or your school canteen, but it should be. Not because it's happening in every school in the most extreme, headline-grabbing ways, but because the roots of it often are. And if we're serious about challenging misogyny in schools, we must be serious about understanding the wider landscape that normalises, excuses, or even enables harm towards women and girls because schools are not separate from that landscape. They are part of it.

It's easy to think of MVAWG as someone else's problem; that it's something for the police to deal with, or a 'home issue' that doesn't fall under our remit. But the reality is that many girls experience their first encounter with harassment, control, coercion, or sexual violence before they even leave full-time education. Many boys, too, start absorbing messages about power, entitlement, and gender early: from their peers, their phones, or the unspoken rules of their environment. What happens (or doesn't happen) in school plays a major role in shaping what they believe is normal.

As I mentioned in the introduction to this book, the National Police Chief's Council called Violence Against Women and Girls an 'epidemic'.[4] But what does that actually mean for us, in schools, on the ground?

This chapter attempts to answer that question. It looks at what MVAWG is and how schools can better prevent it, identify it, and respond to it. It also explores the ways in which our school cultures, language, policies, and blind spots can unintentionally reinforce the very attitudes we're trying to challenge. It's not about turning teachers into police officers or therapists. It's about helping us all – as educators, leaders, and human beings – to better understand the role we play in a bigger picture.

If we're teaching boys that kindness matters and girls that their voices count, then we're already halfway there. But if we're turning a blind eye to the jokes, the comments, the power dynamics, or if we're unsure how to respond when something serious does happen, then we're not there yet. This chapter is written in the belief that schools can be transformative spaces. And to get there, we need to be brave enough to name the problem.

What Is MVAWG? Defining the Problem

MVAWG isn't a single behaviour or crime; it exists along a spectrum. It's the outcome of a culture where male power is normalised, where women and girls are too often expected to absorb discomfort for the sake of peace, and where many forms of harm are so common they're no longer even recognised as harm.

It's often the case that when people hear the phrase 'violence against women and girls', they think immediately of the extreme: rape, murder, domestic abuse. But focusing only on the most horrific outcomes can lead us to overlook the daily behaviours, attitudes, and assumptions that lie further down the spectrum: behaviours that can and do show up in school corridors, WhatsApp groups, and classroom conversations.

The government defines VAWG as 'acts of violence or abuse that we know disproportionately affect women and girls'.[5] That definition includes both *physical* and *non-physical* forms of violence. So, what's included in this spectrum of MVAWG?

The Spectrum of MVAWG

1. **Domestic Abuse**

    This includes not just physical violence but also emotional abuse, economic control, and coercive behaviour within intimate or family relationships. Figures from the ONS show that in 2024, 'Women were disproportionately represented as victims of domestic abuse-related crimes, as in previous years, with 72.5% of all victims being female.'[6] In domestic abuse cases, 93% of defendants are male.[7]

2. **Sexual Violence**

    This covers rape, sexual assault, and unwanted sexual contact. Most victims are women, and most perpetrators are men. Findings from the National Audit Office found in the year ending 2023, 97% of perpetrators of sexual offences against women were male.[8] The same report found that over one in four women will be a victim of sexual assault or attempted assault in their lifetimes. And the conviction rate remains startlingly low: in England, under 1% of reported rapes lead to conviction.[9]

3. **Coercive Control**

    Often harder to identify than physical violence, coercive control refers to behaviours designed to dominate and isolate a victim: things like monitoring someone's phone, controlling what they wear, or limiting their access to money or friends. It's now recognised in UK law as a criminal offence under section 76 of the Serious Crime Act 2015.[10]

4. **Sexual Harassment**

    Unwanted comments, gestures, or touches, many of which happen in school settings. As has already been acknowledged, Ofsted found that 92% of girls and 74% of boys said that sexist name-calling and rumours happened 'a lot' or 'sometimes' in school.[11] Most of these incidents were never formally reported.

5. **Online Abuse and Image-Based Harassment**

    This includes sending unsolicited sexual images, pressuring someone into sending nudes, revenge porn, stalking through social media, and creating deepfake pornography. A 2023 study by Refuge found that one in seven young women had received threats from a partner to share intimate images of them.[12]

6. **Honour-Based Abuse, Forced Marriage, and Female Genital Mutilation (FGM)**

Though less commonly encountered in most school settings, these are forms of MVAWG that some girls are at direct risk of, and schools have a legal safeguarding duty to identify and respond to them.[13] FGM alone affects an estimated 137,000 women and girls in England and Wales.[14]

The Continuum of Harm

These behaviours don't all carry the same legal weight, but they do sit on a continuum that stretches from sexualised joking about girls and women in the playground to femicide; from a Year 9 boy rating girls out of ten in class to a girl being too frightened to break up with her controlling boyfriend; from a raised fist that never lands to a broken jaw and a black eye.

When we minimise so-called 'lesser' acts of MVAWG, we create space for bigger harms to flourish. When schools ignore sexualised 'banter' or dismiss misogynistic behaviour as 'just lads being lads', we reinforce the idea that women's discomfort is a fair price to pay for boys' amusement or dominance.

What Does This Mean for Schools?

We must accept that MVAWG is a school problem. It doesn't necessarily mean that our schools are unsafe or overrun with abuse. It *is* about recognising that gendered power dynamics are everywhere, and if we don't name them, we can't change them.

Many boys and young men don't see themselves as part of the problem because the harm often doesn't look like violence to them. But if we wait until it does, it's already too late. What's needed is a shift in how we talk about these issues: a shift that places power, gender, and responsibility at the centre. That starts with seeing MVAWG not just as a criminal justice issue but as a cultural and educational one. One that requires us – as teachers, leaders, and adults in young people's lives – to take it seriously early, consistently, and collectively.

MVAWG in the Classroom

Male violence against women and girls doesn't start with a clenched fist thrown in anger. It starts long before that, with control, with entitlement, and with a slow erosion of a girl's sense of autonomy. And while schools may not be the place where the most serious harm occurs, they're often the place where the foundations of MVAWG are laid.

Many young men who go on to abuse or control partners don't see themselves as violent. They see themselves as protective, passionate, assertive, or 'just a bloke'. That's because the cultural cues that shape male violence are often normalised from a young age, and schools, if we're not careful, can be one of the places where those cues are rehearsed and reinforced. Let's look at some of the ways MVAWG reveals itself in schools.

1. Control Framed as Romance

One of the most common precursors to later abuse is coercive control and it rarely looks violent at the start. It looks like a boyfriend who wants to know where his girlfriend is all the time. Who gets angry when she posts on Instagram. Who insists on walking her home and to and from each of her lessons. Who comments about her clothes. Who tells her that other boys are only being nice to her because they want something.

In schools, this kind of behaviour is often minimised or, worse, romanticised. It's not unusual to hear staff and students say things

Male Violence Against Women and Girls

like *'He's just really into her'* or *'They're inseparable.'* But being inseparable isn't always about closeness. Sometimes it's about possession.

If a 15-year-old boy expects total access to his girlfriend's phone, or tells her not to speak to other boys, or repeatedly demands to know where she is, that's not puppy love. That's a potential rehearsal for greater levels of coercive control.

2. Emotional Bullying

Some boys are openly competitive over girls, treating relationships as territory, not connection. You'll hear comments like *'She's mine'*, *'I had her first'*, or *'He's trying to move to my girl.'* In these situations, girls become a status symbol, a possession: something to win, keep, and guard.

When those dynamics play out in real time, they're often subtle. A girl crying in the corridor. A boy sulking after seeing her laugh with someone else. A quiet standoff in the canteen. It rarely looks like violence. But it often feels like fear.

We need to be alert to these dynamics not only for safeguarding reasons but for educational ones. We need to help boys unlearn the idea that emotional control is romantic, and help girls recognise that love shouldn't feel like walking on eggshells.

3. The 'Hard Man' Persona

In schools where toughness is part of the masculine currency, boys who posture as 'hard' or aggressive often command social respect. These are the boys who shout across corridors, bang desks, or stare other students down. They're not always violent in school, but they carry a kind of implied threat: the sense that they *could* be.

Girls who date these boys might feel flattered by the attention, at least at first. But the risk is that intimidation, volatility, and unpredictability get absorbed as normal features of male behaviour. Over time, this creates a model of masculinity that links power with fear. This combination sits at the heart of domestic abuse.

Schools need to challenge the myth that some boys are just naturally 'like that'. Because that myth, when left unchallenged, becomes a shield for abuse.

4. Violence Against Other Boys as a Red Flag

Not all boys who are violent towards girls show those tendencies at school. But many do show early warning signs in how they treat other boys, particularly those they see as weaker, soft, or unmanly. These behaviours might be brushed off as bullying or banter, but they often reflect deeper beliefs about dominance, entitlement, and strength. When boys rely on violence or intimidation to gain respect, they're often rehearsing the same power dynamics that underpin intimate partner violence later in life.[15] Recognising this isn't about labelling students as future abusers: it's about early intervention, emotional education, and giving them alternative scripts before those behaviours become entrenched.

5. What Girls Don't Say (and Why)

Perhaps the most important thing to recognise is silence.

Girls rarely report controlling or abusive behaviour unless it becomes unbearable and even then, many don't. Sometimes they worry about the consequences. Sometimes they think they won't be believed. More often, they just don't recognise what's happening to them as abuse because it doesn't look like what they've been taught abuse looks like.

They might say, *'He just gets jealous,'* or *'He's a bit full-on but that's just how he is.'* They might stop seeing friends, delete social media, change how they dress. They might smile and say everything's

Male Violence Against Women and Girls

fine while navigating an entire relationship that feels more like surveillance than love.

A Culture of Control

MVAWG in schools doesn't usually look like violence. It looks like control disguised as care, like jealousy excused as love, like possessiveness mistaken for passion. Because it often hides behind these familiar ideas, it can be hard to name and even harder to challenge.

But naming it is exactly what we need to do. Because if we want to prevent future harm, we can't wait for bruises. We have to start by dismantling the beliefs and behaviours that make violence seem like a natural extension of love, masculinity, or status. Schools aren't the whole solution, but they can be a powerful part of it.

Recognising the Warning Signs

When it comes to MVAWG, schools are rarely the site of the most visible or extreme incidents, but they are often where the warning signs first emerge. Part of the difficulty is that these signs don't always look like violence, especially when they're playing out in teenage relationships or between boys trying to perform a certain version of masculinity. In a busy school environment, where staff are under pressure and students are still working out who they are, it's easy to overlook the patterns that matter most.

We need to be observant, reflective, and open to the possibility that what we're seeing (or not seeing) could point to something deeper.

What to Look for in Girls at Risk

Girls experiencing early forms of coercive control or abuse often don't disclose it, not because they're hiding it, but because they

Unmasking the Manosphere

think it's normal, believe it's their fault, or confuse control with care. That means the signs are often subtle.

Signs that may indicate a girl is at risk of MVAWG:

- **Withdrawal** from friends, clubs, or social spaces they used to enjoy.
- **Changes in appearance**: dressing differently (more modestly, more covered up), often at the request of a partner.
- **Increased phone anxiety**: jumping to reply to texts, looking visibly tense when they receive notifications.
- **Frequent checking in with a boyfriend**: even during lessons or break times.
- **Making excuses for controlling behaviour**: e.g. *'He just gets jealous'* or *'He doesn't like it when I'm around other boys.'*
- **Sudden drops in confidence**: especially if the girl was previously vocal, sociable, or high achieving.

You may also notice that a girl in this situation stops engaging in conversations about relationships, feminism, or gender because it's suddenly become too close to home.

What to Look for in Boys Showing Concerning Patterns

Again, it's rarely the outright aggression that shows up first

Early signs that a boy might be a perpetrator of MVAWG might include:

- **Extreme jealousy**: visible discomfort when their girlfriend talks to other boys or an obsessive focus on her whereabouts.
- **Attempts to isolate**: encouraging her to stop speaking to certain friends or avoid social situations.
- **Controlling behaviour** framed as care: e.g. *'I just worry about you too much'* or *'I only get like this because I love you.'*
- **Monitoring her phone/social media**: pressuring for passwords, checking who she follows or messages.

- **Rehearsal of violent or threatening language**: particularly in jokes, arguments, or chats with other boys.
- **Disregard for rules or boundaries**: especially when they don't get their own way.

It's important to note that not all boys who display these signs will go on to become abusive partners, but many abusive men started with exactly this pattern of entitlement, control, and emotional volatility.

Warning Signs in Peer Dynamics and Friendship Groups

Often the red flags are visible not just in individuals but in the culture around them. Schools that struggle with unchallenged sexism, 'hard man' hierarchies, or normalised disrespect towards girls tend to see clusters of these behaviours, not just isolated cases.

Things to watch out for:

- **Group chats** where boys rate girls, share private images, or joke about violence.
- **Girls expressing fear or discomfort around certain boys** even if they won't say why.
- **Boys backing each other up when called out**: defensiveness, group denial, or victim blaming.
- **A culture of silence**: students saying things like *'Nothing ever happens'* or *'It's not worth reporting'*.

Staff Blind Spots and the Risk of Misinterpretation

Many early signs of MVAWG-related behaviour are subtle and can easily be misread, especially if the student involved is 'popular', academically able, or outwardly respectful to staff.

We might:

- Dismiss a boy's controlling tendencies as 'being overprotective'

Unmasking the Manosphere

- See a girl's withdrawal as typical teen moodiness
- Overlook power imbalances in relationships because 'they seem loved-up'
- Accept manipulative behaviour as 'he's just struggling emotionally' without examining its impact

This is why it's crucial we talk about MVAWG openly in staffrooms and safeguarding meetings because recognising these signs requires shared language, shared expectations, and a willingness to name what we're seeing.

Seeing What's There

Recognising the warning signs of MVAWG-related behaviours isn't about treating students with suspicion. It's about noticing when something doesn't sit right. It's about listening to silences, watching patterns, and challenging ourselves to look again when a dynamic feels off. No one expects teachers to diagnose abuse. But we can learn to spot what might be coming, and when we do, we can step in early, offer support, and shift the story before it becomes a statistic.

What Schools Need to Do About MVAWG

As teachers, it often feels that in addition to teaching coastal sea erosion, trigonometry, and sonnets, we are also expected to be police officers, social workers, or trauma therapists. And that's before we even get to think about endless piles of marking, meetings about other meetings, and break duties. But the truth is, we *are* educators, role models, gatekeepers of culture, and adults in a position to notice when something isn't right. Like a certain arachnid superhero, this gives us a huge amount of power and responsibility when it comes to preventing male violence, identifying risk, and responding appropriately when concerns arise.

Male Violence Against Women and Girls

Schools' efforts to combat MVAWG can be broken down into three distinct parts: **Prevention**, **Identification**, and **Response**.

PREVENTION

1. Whole-School Culture

The most powerful tool a school has in the fight against MVAWG is its culture.

If boys are taught, explicitly and implicitly, that their power is natural and unchallengeable, they will carry that assumption with them into relationships. If girls are taught to keep the peace, stay quiet, and tolerate discomfort, they may not even notice when control turns into coercion. Creating a culture where power is accountable, boundaries are respected, and consent is understood doesn't start in PSHE. It starts in every corridor, every classroom, every adult interaction.

That means:

- Staff consistently responding to controlling or demeaning behaviour
- High expectations of respectful conduct between students
- Zero tolerance for romanticising control or jealousy
- Language policies that challenge gendered slurs and threats

When this is done well, schools stop becoming environments where abuse is rehearsed and start becoming places where equality is practised.

2. Involving Boys Without Alienating Them

Boys need to be part of the conversation. Not because they're all potential perpetrators, but because many of them will witness, challenge, excuse, or ignore harmful behaviour in their peer groups.

Unmasking the Manosphere

That involvement should focus on:

- Understanding power and entitlement
- Reframing masculinity
- Creating space for empathy, accountability, and change
- Holding other men to account (see Chapter 4 and the *Come Off It* method)

Approaches like mentorship schemes, peer education, and student-led projects can be effective, particularly when they centre boys as potential allies and not just risks.

IDENTIFICATION

Schools are often the first place changes show up: a girl becomes withdrawn, a boy starts exhibiting possessiveness, friendship groups shift. But those signs are only useful if someone's looking out for them.

1. Knowing What to Look For

Staff should be confident in recognising:

- Early controlling behaviour
- Emotional volatility and possessiveness
- Withdrawal, shame, or sudden personality shifts
- Disrespectful peer dynamics

It's also about knowing that one-off incidents are rarely just one off. If something feels uncomfortable, we need to ask: *is this part of a pattern?*

2. Encouraging Disclosure Without Forcing It

Girls don't always want to talk and when they do, it's usually to someone they trust.

Male Violence Against Women and Girls

To make disclosure more likely:

- Build strong relationships, especially between students and pastoral staff
- Create multiple, accessible routes to report concerns
- Publicly promote a 'tell someone' culture without centring punishment

Even a single sentence from a student, for example, *'He checks my phone every night,'* should be taken seriously. That kind of control is often the tip of the iceberg.

3. Being Proactive, Not Passive

Waiting until violence is visible is too late. Schools can proactively:

- Check in with students whose relationships raise concern
- Encourage safe conversations in PSHE
- Watch for patterns in attendance, performance, and wellbeing data
- Include coercive control and relationship red flags in safeguarding briefings

RESPONSE

When a student does disclose, or when a staff member raises a concern, the school's response matters, not just for the student in question but for the whole culture.

1. Trauma-Informed Practice

A trauma-informed response doesn't mean soft. It means being sensitive, clear, and non-judgemental.

That includes:

- Listening without shock, blame, or disbelief
- Avoiding 'why didn't you…' questions

Unmasking the Manosphere

- Offering choices – about who they speak to, when, and what happens next
- Making clear what can and can't be kept confidential

Every disclosure is an act of bravery. Our job is to meet it with care.

2. Working with External Agencies

MVAWG cases may require referrals to:

- Social services
- The police (if a crime has occurred)
- Local domestic abuse support services
- CAMHS or counselling services

Schools shouldn't be afraid to involve specialists. But equally, they should remain involved, offering consistent pastoral support, check-ins, and advocacy where needed.

Disciplinary Action and Restorative Approaches

Serious abuse or violence should never be handled *only* through restorative justice. But schools do need clarity on how to discipline in a way that:

- Holds perpetrators accountable
- Ensures safety for others
- Doesn't send a message that boys can intimidate or harm without real consequence

A strong behaviour policy, linked explicitly to safeguarding and equality, can help here.

Culture Is the Intervention

The most effective response to MVAWG is to build a school environment where it simply doesn't belong. That takes work. It takes consistency. It takes honest reflection about what we overlook, excuse, or deny.

But it's possible. And it starts not with big gestures but with everyday actions: calling things out, listening properly, believing in students, supporting staff, and recognising that prevention isn't an extra but part of the job.

When schools lead with courage and clarity, the difference is real: not just for girls but for everyone who grows up watching how power is handled.

Using the Curriculum to Tackle MVAWG

Pastoral work is crucial, but it's only half the picture. If we want to prevent MVAWG, we have to look at what's being taught in the classroom and, perhaps more importantly, what isn't.

The curriculum is where values are embedded, where beliefs are reinforced or challenged, and where students learn how to make sense of the world and absorb ideas and beliefs about gender, power, and relationships. When schools are intentional about using the curriculum to tackle the attitudes that underpin MVAWG, the impact can be profound.

This isn't about ticking boxes or shoehorning MVAWG into every lesson. It's about using what we're already teaching to open space for reflection, empathy, and critical thinking.

1. English: Power, Gender, and Control in Texts

English is uniquely placed to explore coercion, violence, and power dynamics.

Opportunities include:

- Studying toxic male entitlement in texts like *Othello*, *An Inspector Calls*, *A Streetcar Named Desire*, or *Of Mice and Men*

Unmasking the Manosphere

- Analysing coercive control in modern literature texts such as *Pigeon English*, *Noughts and Crosses*, or *Purple Hibiscus*
- Exploring the language of dominance and shame by analysing how male characters talk *about* women vs how they talk *to* women
- Comparing character arcs of men who use violence with those who take responsibility or change
- Creative writing tasks that subvert traditional gender narratives or explore the emotional cost of control

2. PSHE/RSE: Moving Beyond Consent

A lot of schools deliver content on *consent*, but it's often framed too narrowly and too late. It's not enough to say 'no means no' if students have already absorbed messages that equate love with possession or jealousy with passion.

RSE can tackle MVAWG more directly by:

- Teaching the signs of coercive control as well as physical abuse
- Exploring how 'nice guys' can still be abusive when entitlement is at play
- Showing how emotional manipulation, gaslighting, and guilt-tripping work
- Using real-world scenarios, case studies, and anonymised examples
- Explicitly challenging the idea that violence is ever proof of love

Boys, in particular, need space to explore:

- How emotional control gets disguised as romance
- Why many abusers don't *see* themselves as violent
- What healthier models of masculinity can look like

And girls need space to name:

- The difference between 'protective' and 'possessive'

- How to spot red flags early
- That their intuition and discomfort are valid

3. History: Contextualising Power and Patriarchy

History classrooms can help students understand that MVAWG doesn't appear out of nowhere; that it's woven into the way power has operated for centuries.

Ideas to explore:

- The legal history of male ownership over women (e.g. marital rape law)
- Case studies of feminist resistance (e.g. the Suffragettes, Reclaim the Night, the Women's Liberation Movement)
- How domestic violence has been addressed (or ignored) across time
- The role institutions in law, medicine, and religion have played in excusing male violence
- Comparative global approaches to women's rights and gender-based violence

Encouraging students to analyse systems, not just events, creates a stronger foundation for understanding how male violence becomes normalised and how it can be undone.

4. Drama: Rehearsing Empathy and Power Shifts

Drama is an ideal space to explore emotional control, status, threat, and vulnerability.

Opportunities include:

- Forum theatre techniques to rehearse responses to abusive behaviour

- Role-playing power dynamics in intimate relationships or friendship groups
- Exploring how characters justify, excuse, or deny harmful actions
- Creating original performances around the theme of control and its impact
- Exploring body dynamics and body language and its role in relationship dynamics

It's also an excellent space for boys to explore the *emotional* cost of dominance and for all students to practise calling out harmful behaviour safely and confidently. Perhaps get students to practise the *Come Off It* method here!

5. Media/Sociology/Politics: Deconstructing Influence

These subjects are crucial for helping students question the media and online environments that often shape their beliefs more than school ever could.

Use lessons to explore:

- How male violence is represented in news, film, music, and gaming
- Who gets sympathy in true crime narratives: the male perpetrator or the female victim?
- The difference between male anger and female fear as cultural narratives
- Political responses to MVAWG
- The rise of influencer culture and how figures like Andrew Tate promote misogyny under the banner of masculinity

Encouraging students to unpick *why* some forms of violence are glorified, minimised, or justified helps them become more resistant to dangerous messages elsewhere.

Male Violence Against Women and Girls

6. *Science and PE: Unexpected but Important Spaces*

In science:

- Highlight the gender gap in medical research, including the dismissal of women's pain
- Discuss how hormones are wrongly used to justify aggression in boys or emotional instability in girls
- Explore the neurobiology of fear, trauma, and stress, especially in relation to abusive environments

In PE:

- Challenge the myth that strength equals dominance
- Celebrate male athletes who model care, compassion, and respect (e.g. Marcus Rashford, Mo Farah, Tom Daley)
- Promote sportsmanship and teamwork over rivalry and control
- Tackle homophobic and misogynistic language in changing rooms and team banter

Every subject has a role to play, and sometimes the most unexpected ones leave the deepest impression.

Curriculum as Culture

What we choose to teach and how we choose to teach it tells students who matters, what matters, and what behaviours are normal. If MVAWG prevention work is confined to a single RSE lesson or safeguarding poster, we miss the deeper opportunity: to help young people make sense of gender, power, and relationships across every part of their learning. The curriculum isn't just what students learn. It's what they carry. Let's make sure we're helping them carry something worth holding on to.

Working with Parents and the Wider Community

When schools take a strong stance on MVAWG there's often a degree of apprehension: *How will parents react? Will we be accused of blaming boys? What happens if someone complains?* These are valid concerns. But if we're serious about reducing MVAWG, we can't do it in a vacuum. We need to bring families and the wider community with us in order to reinforce what we're doing in school, and also because many of the most dangerous messages about gender, control, and violence come from *outside* the school gates.

Engaging parents doesn't mean asking them to be experts. It means helping them understand why this work matters, how they can support it, and what they need to be aware of, both online and offline.

1. Be Clear, Not Confrontational

One of the most effective ways to avoid backlash is to be clear and calm about what we're doing and why. We're not accusing boys. We're not saying all men are violent. We're not promoting an ideology. We're teaching students how to build relationships based on respect, not control.

Communications to parents should:

- Use plain language: *'We're helping students understand what healthy relationships look like, and how to recognise behaviours that might feel unsafe or controlling.'*
- Explain the data: *'Most violence against women and girls is perpetrated by men and we want to be part of preventing that by starting early.'*
- Reassure them that all students benefit in the fight against MVAWG: boys, girls, non-binary students. Everyone deserves to feel safe and heard.

Male Violence Against Women and Girls

When we communicate confidently and transparently, most parents understand, while those who disagree are less likely to escalate if they feel respected, not lectured.

2. Anticipate and Address Misunderstandings

Common points of friction include: *'Why are you teaching my son that he's a potential abuser?' 'This is political – it's not appropriate for schools.' 'What happened to teaching reading and maths?'*

It helps to:

- Pre-empt these reactions in your FAQs or letters home
- Frame the work as part of safeguarding and character education
- Emphasise the long-term benefits: reduced harm, healthier relationships, more respectful classrooms
- Offer parent drop-ins or webinars where staff can explain the approach in more depth

Most resistance doesn't come from malice but from fear or from people feeling left out of the conversation. Invite them in.

3. Signpost, Don't Shame

Some families may have personal experience with domestic abuse, coercive control, or harmful gender norms. Others may simply not have the tools or language to talk about these things at home.

Rather than shaming or judging, schools can:

- Signpost resources such as Refuge, Women's Aid, the *Love Respect* site for young people, or NSPCC's *Talk PANTS* for younger children
- Share guides on talking to children about relationships, jealousy, online safety, or warning signs of control
- Offer pastoral support or referrals if needed

Unmasking the Manosphere

The goal isn't to turn every parent into a gender specialist. It's to empower them to have the conversations their child might not otherwise hear.

4. *Challenge Gently, but Firmly*

Some parents may hold views that contradict your school's values – for example, normalising male control, minimising violence, or policing girls' behaviour instead of challenging boys'.

This may show up in comments like: *'Well, what was she wearing?' 'He's only like that because he cares so much.' 'That's just how boys are.'*

When this happens, it's important to:

- Stick to your values: make clear that your school does not tolerate victim blaming or minimising abuse
- Avoid personal attacks: focus on the impact of the behaviour, not the parent's character
- Redirect to safeguarding: reinforce that your approach is based on national guidance and your duty to protect all students as outlined in *Keeping Children Safe in Education*

You won't change every mind, but you can create a clear boundary around what your school stands for.

5. *Build Partnerships with Local Organisations*

Your school doesn't have to do this work alone.

Forge links with:

- Local domestic abuse services who can deliver workshops, assemblies, or staff training
- Women's centres or youth outreach projects

- Police School Liaison Officers (provided their approach is trauma informed and preventative)
- Faith and community leaders who can help contextualise the work in different cultural settings

Bringing in external voices can reinforce your message as well as give students more ways to seek help if they need it.

6. Go Beyond the Gate

Preventing MVAWG isn't just about what happens in lessons; it's also about safety on the walk home, in the park after school, or on social media after dark.

Schools can:

- Advocate for safe walking routes, better street lighting, or safer transport
- Work with local authorities to reduce environmental risk (e.g. alleyways near schools, isolated bus stops)
- Share community alerts around high-risk individuals or areas
- Offer parent sessions on digital abuse, controlling behaviours, and how to talk to children about relationships

When students see schools active in the wider community, it sends a message: your safety matters everywhere, not just in school hours.

Invite In, Don't Lock Out

We don't win hearts or shift cultures by shutting parents out. And when it comes to MVAWG, silence is a luxury we can't afford. Parents and communities might not always say it in the same language, but many of them *do* want their children to grow up in a world where love doesn't hurt and power doesn't get abused. By working together, we stand a much better chance of turning that hope into something real.

Looking Inward: How School Cultures Can Unwittingly Enable Misogyny

One of the hardest truths to face in this work is that schools – even progressive, high-achieving, inclusive ones – can quietly reinforce the very dynamics that enable male violence against women and girls. Not because anyone intends harm or because the staff aren't committed or the leadership is uninterested, but because so much of what enables MVAWG sits beneath the surface. It lives in the assumptions we don't question, the jokes we ignore, the double standards we accept, and the silences we fall into.

Tackling male violence isn't just about identifying risks in students. It's also about examining the culture of the adults and the systems surrounding them.

1. The Staffroom: Banter, Bias, and Blind Spots

The tone of a school is often set in the staffroom and that includes the tone around gender.

Sometimes it's overt: a joke about a 'high maintenance' female colleague, a dismissive comment about feminism, or a remark about what a girl was wearing in the corridor. Other times, it's more subtle: disbelief when a boy is accused of controlling behaviour (*'Really? He's so polite'*) or sympathy skewed towards male students in safeguarding cases (*'He must be heartbroken'*). None of this makes someone a bad teacher. But it does shape how seriously we take disclosures, how we interpret behaviour, and who we instinctively defend.

Reflective schools create space to ask:

- *What kinds of jokes do we let pass unchallenged?*
- *Whose perspectives do we prioritise in safeguarding meetings?*
- *Do we believe some students more easily than others? If so, why?*

Male Violence Against Women and Girls

Creating a safe culture for students means creating a safe culture for staff too. A culture where people can question assumptions without fear of embarrassment or backlash.

2. Double Standards in Behaviour Policies

Sometimes the school's own policies can reinforce gendered expectations without meaning to. Common examples include:

- Girls being punished for their reaction, not the provocation, e.g. a girl gets detention for shouting at a boy who's been harassing her for weeks
- Stricter uniform enforcement for girls, e.g. focusing on skirt length or makeup in a way that implies their appearance is a disruption
- Language that centres girls' behaviour or appearance as the problem, e.g. *'You need to be careful what message you're sending'* or *'Don't give him the wrong idea'.*

This isn't about being overly critical of staff. It's about recognising how embedded these scripts are in our systems and how they shape what we see as 'normal' or 'acceptable'.

A gender-aware approach means:

- Reviewing policies for bias
- Looking at who gets referred for behaviour issues and what behaviours are being punished
- Asking whether discipline is reinforcing the very power dynamics we're trying to dismantle

3. Safeguarding Gaps and Inconsistent Follow-Through

Safeguarding procedures are often solid on paper but inconsistent in practice.

Issues include:

- Disclosures not being escalated because they 'don't meet threshold'
- Concerns about controlling relationships being deprioritised because there's no physical abuse
- Lack of follow-up after a student has shared something serious
- No cross-checking of patterns, e.g. a boy with multiple low-level concerns raised by different staff, none of which are seen as connected

Of course, these aren't malicious oversights. They're system-level issues caused by pressure, limited time, and under-resourcing, but the result is the same: girls not being protected, and boys not being challenged.

A more robust safeguarding culture around MVAWG means:

- Treating coercive control as a red flag, not a grey area
- Creating systems to join the dots between pastoral, academic, and safeguarding teams
- Making sure 'he's just struggling' doesn't become a reason to overlook someone else's harm

4. Role Models and Representation

Who gets celebrated in school culture? Who's held up as an example? Who do students see as respected adults?

If a school's male role models are all high-status, traditionally masculine figures – disciplinarians, sports coaches, assertive senior leaders – but the compassionate, emotionally intelligent staff are overlooked, we send a message about what masculinity looks like.

Male Violence Against Women and Girls

If girls don't see women in leadership or only hear their voices in safeguarding sessions rather than assemblies or curriculum content, the same message applies.

Challenging MVAWG includes:

- Broadening who we showcase and celebrate
- Inviting men to model care, reflection, and vulnerability – not just strength and control
- Ensuring female staff aren't expected to do all the emotional labour around gender, behaviour, and wellbeing

5. Emotional Safety for Staff Who Challenge the Culture

There are often one or two members of staff in every school who *do* see the problems, raise concerns, and challenge inappropriate comments. But too often, they end up isolated.

If schools are serious about tackling MVAWG, they need to protect and support these staff. That means:

- Backing them up when they challenge students or colleagues
- Listening when they flag patterns others have missed
- Recognising that pushing for cultural change can be exhausting *and* lonely

Change doesn't come from one passionate staff member. It comes from leadership standing beside them and saying: *We see it too. And we're with you.*

Most schools aren't ignoring MVAWG out of malice. They're just busy, overstretched, and unsure where to start. But recognising where culture might be enabling or excusing harmful attitudes is a powerful first step. It's about creating an environment where everyone within the school community understands that power without reflection can be dangerous. When we look inward, honestly and bravely, we lay the groundwork for real, lasting change.

The Final Word

MVAWG is not a fringe issue. It's not something that exists only in crime statistics, or behind closed doors, or in the lives of other people. It's in our schools: in the culture, in the corridors, in the way power and gender are understood (or not understood) by the young people we teach every day. But the question is not just *'What do we do about it?'* It's *'Why does this matter to us as educators?'* The answer, for me, is simple: because education is moral work.

We are not just teaching facts and figures. We're shaping citizens. We're creating environments that tell students who matters, whose voice counts, and what kind of behaviour will be tolerated. We're drawing lines, constantly, around what's acceptable, what's harmful, and what kind of person it's okay to become.

And that means we cannot be neutral on this.

To ignore the conditions that allow male violence to grow by pretending they don't exist or by avoiding the discomfort of naming them is to quietly accept them. And in accepting them, we fail the girls in our care, but we also fail the boys. Boys deserve more than a version of masculinity that ties their worth to control, or fear, or dominance. They deserve the tools to build relationships based on equality. They deserve to know that anger is not the only language they're allowed to speak and they deserve adults who believe they are capable of change.

This isn't easy work. It's hard, often unrewarded, and sometimes lonely. But it matters more than we realise. Because when we get this right; when we create a culture where control is recognised,

Male Violence Against Women and Girls

where violence is not normalised, and where silence is no longer the default, we create something powerful.

We create a school where girls feel safe walking through the gates and where boys are free to unlearn the worst messages they've inherited. A school that doesn't just *teach* equality but lives it.

We won't always get it right, but every conversation we start, every behaviour we challenge, every silence we break all make a difference. This work doesn't belong to a safeguarding lead, or a PSHE coordinator, or one passionate member of staff. It belongs to all of us.

Notes

1. Although I use MVAWG, I retain the use of the term VAWG when referencing other people or institutions who use that term in their own literature
2. www.womensaid.org.uk/information-support/what-is-domestic-abuse/domestic-abuse-is-a-gendered-crime/.
3. https://rapecrisis.org.uk/get-informed/about-sexual-violence/myths-vs-realities/
4. https://news.npcc.police.uk/releases/call-to-action-as-violence-against-women-and-girls-epidemic-deepens-1
5. www.gov.uk/government/publications/tackling-violence-against-women-and-girls-strategy
6. www.ons.gov.uk/peoplepopulationandcommunity/crimeandjustice/bulletins/domesticabuseinenglandandwalesoverview/november2024
7. https://refuge.org.uk/what-is-domestic-abuse/the-facts/
8. www.nao.org.uk/reports/tackling-violence-against-women-and-girls/
9. www.citystgeorges.ac.uk/news-and-events/news/2022/04/new-scorecards-show-under-1-of-reported-rapes-lead-to-conviction-criminologist-explains-why-englands-justice-system-continues-to-fail
10. www.legislation.gov.uk/ukpga/2015/9/section/76
11. www.gov.uk/government/publications/review-of-sexual-abuse-in-schools-and-colleges
12. https://refuge.org.uk/wp-content/uploads/2020/07/The-Naked-Threat-Report.pdf

13. www.gov.uk/government/publications/keeping-children-safe-in-education--2
14. City University London (2015). *Prevalence of female genital mutilation in England and Wales.*
15. Ehrensaft, M. K., Cohen, P., Brown, J., Smailes, E., Chen, H., & Johnson, J. G. (2003). Intergenerational transmission of partner violence: A 20-year prospective study. *Journal of Consulting and Clinical Psychology, 71*(4), 741–753. https://doi.org/10.1037/0022-006x.71.4.741

6 The Road Ahead

We've covered a lot of ground in this book. We've talked about how boys learn misogyny, from playground whispers to algorithm-fed social media spirals. We've looked at the pressures that come with being a boy – how the rules of toughness, emotional suppression, and sexual bravado are passed down like unwanted hand-me-downs. We've unpacked pornography, incel culture, algorithms, the normalisation of sexual harassment, and the way even 'jokes' can reinforce something far more serious. And we've examined how schools, often without meaning to, facilitate the perfect environment for these ideas to fester.

This probably hasn't been comfortable to read. It wasn't comfortable to write, either. But avoiding discomfort is how we got here in the first place. We can't address misogyny by skimming the surface. We must wade into the murky stuff – the things that feel awkward, heated, or too big to fix.

The point of this book has never been to shame boys or vilify men. It's to understand the forces shaping them and to figure out what we, as adults, can do to guide them towards something better. The truth is, most boys don't wake up deciding to be misogynists. They are treading water in an ocean of messages, images, and expectations that normalise inequality. They learn early on what earns approval from peers and what earns ridicule. If those rewards and punishments are rooted in sexism, then sexism will thrive.

The Responsibility of Adults

It is no good pointing the finger at boys and shrugging when they say something sexist in class or share a degrading meme. We have to own the fact that *we are their environment*. Teachers, support staff, and parents are all part of the culture they grow up in. That means we're part of the problem when we stay silent, and we can be part of the solution when we speak up.

This starts with vigilance. Listen to the language boys use around each other. Pay attention to what's being laughed at, what's being dismissed as 'banter', and what's going unchallenged. The quieter the adult response, the louder the harmful norms become.

We also have to be braver about our own learning. The world boys are growing up in is not the same as the one many adults remember. If the last time you thought about pornography in schools was when you confiscated a magazine in 1998, you're behind. If you think 'incel' is just an online joke, you're underestimating a dangerous movement. Keeping up with the culture boys are navigating isn't optional: it's a safeguarding responsibility.

The Responsibility of Schools

Schools are one of the few places where we can reach almost every boy, every day. That's an extraordinary opportunity but also a serious duty. Every school should have a clear, lived approach to tackling sexism and misogyny, and that approach should go far beyond an annual assembly.

The Road Ahead

It means building a culture where sexist language is consistently challenged, where relationships and sex education is honest and relevant, and where boys are encouraged to explore their emotions without shame. It means making sure all staff, from lunchtime supervisors to senior leaders, know what to look for and how to respond. It means having policies that don't just exist in a dusty handbook but actually shape what happens in corridors, changing rooms, and online spaces.

And crucially, it means holding the line. There will be pushback: from students who roll their eyes; from parents who think you're overreacting; from colleagues who say 'boys will be boys'. That's when leadership matters most.

The Responsibility of Parents

Parents are often the most influential role models in a boy's life. That influence can be positive or negative. A boy who sees his father speak respectfully about women, take emotional risks, and reject casual sexism is being shown a different version of masculinity than the one he'll get from TikTok.

But influence doesn't come from being perfect. It comes from being present and willing to talk. It's the father who admits he's learning too. It's the mother who asks questions about what her son is watching online instead of assuming he'll tell her. It's the parent who models apologising when they get it wrong.

Conversations about misogyny, consent, and respect don't need to be one-off 'big talks'. In fact, they're more effective when they're part of the background noise of everyday life: the comments made during a TV show, the questions asked when a news story breaks, the response given when a child says something troubling.

The Responsibility of Boys

And then, of course, there's the boys themselves. What can *they* do? The answer isn't glamorous. It's everyday stuff:

- **Notice their words**: not just the ones they say to girls but the ones they say to each other.
- **Challenge their mates** even when it's awkward.
- **Listen more than they speak** when someone tells them they've been hurt or disrespected.
- **Ask themselves who benefits** when women are treated as less than men, and who loses.
- **Be willing to be different** from what's expected of them, even if it costs them social points.

None of this is about being perfect. It's about paying attention, taking responsibility, and deciding that respect is more important than fitting in with the worst parts of the group.

Hope Is the Engine

One thing I've learned from years of working in schools is that boys can change quickly, dramatically, and permanently, when the conditions are right. I've seen the so-called 'problem lads' become the fiercest defenders of their female classmates after being given a chance to reflect and a safe space to speak. I've seen groups of Year 9 boys police their own language better than some staff once they understood *why* it mattered.

This is why I reject the fatalistic view that misogyny is something we can't change. That kind of thinking is an excuse for doing nothing. Boys are not doomed to repeat the mistakes of the generations before them. But they do need help to question what they've been told, to see beyond the narrow version of masculinity they've inherited, and to practise a better way.

Your Part in This

So, where does that leave us? It leaves us with no illusions about the scale of the problem and no excuses to ignore it. If you're a teacher, start with your classroom. If you're a parent, start with your kitchen table. If you're a coach, start with the next team talk.

You don't have to dismantle the whole system by yourself. You just have to make sure that in *your* corner of the world, sexism is not the default. That the boys you influence leave your presence with more respect for women, not less. That you model the courage you want them to have.

The Final Word

Culture is not fixed. It is a living thing, made and remade every day by the words we choose, the actions we take, and the things we let slide. If we want a culture where boys grow into men who see women as equals, we have to build it: in classrooms, in living rooms, on pitches, and online.

The work will be messy. It will be tiring. You will sometimes feel like you're getting nowhere. But every conversation you have, every harmful joke you challenge, every piece of harmful media you help a boy think critically about, all adds up.

And one day, one of those boys will look back and realise you were part of the reason he became the man he is. That's not just worth the effort. That's the point.

Index

5Ds Model of Bystander Intervention 92–97, 105
80:20 principle 21–22

age of consent 86
'aggrieved entitlement' 27
Alana's Involuntary Celibacy Project website 23
algorithms 55–56, 61; understanding 66
alpha males 25–26, 42
ambivalence, as part of misogyny discussion process 123
anxiety 27, 34, 37
appearance, making sexual/degrading comments about 113
assault by penetration offence 86
attitudes: influencers' impact on 57–58; pornography impact on 51–55
avoidance of tackling sexist incidents 120–121

banter 47, 56, 75, 82, 83, 87, 104, 135; challenging 110, 112; misogyny as 117; staffroom 156
'Beckies' 24
behaviour policies 10; double standards in 157
beta males 25

bias, teacher 1–2, 156
black pill ideology 21, 28, 32
blaming, victim 4, 76, 77
blindspots 141–142, 156
blue and red pill ideology 20–21
'Boys will be boys' 5, 76, 77; rejection of 48
Bridges, A. J. 52
bullying 6; emotional 137

caring role models 48
'Chads' 24
child sexual abuse 7, 11
child-on-adult sexual harassment 10, 79–82
Children's Commissioner 51–52
coercive control 60, 134, 136–137, 139–140, 147–148
Come Off It method 97–98, 105
communications to parents 152–153
community involvement 152–155
conditioning 28
connecting boys to school community 69–71
consent 64, 85, 86–87
contact forms of harmful sexual behaviour 7
control 140, 141; coercive 60, 134, 136–137, 139–140; culture of 139; framed as romance 136–137

Index

conversation starters 65, 72
Cooper, M. 106–110
counter-narratives: creation of 73; lack of exposure to 103
critical thinkers, building 60–63
cucks 26
cultural norms 103
culture 167; of control 139; curriculum as 151; staffroom 156–157, whole-school *see* whole-school culture
curiosity, as part of misogyny discussion process 122–123
curiosity about sex, normalisation of 65
curriculum 147–151
currycel 35

dating app profiles 22–23
Davison, J. 31–32, 33
delay (5Ds of Bystander Intervention) 94–95, 105
delegation (5Ds of Bystander Intervention) 93, 105
Department for Education (DfE) 104; *Keeping Children Safe in Education* 8–9, 81, 83–86, 87–88, 154
depressive symptoms 27, 34, 37
direct intervention 95–96, 97, 105
disciplinary action 146
disclosure *see* reporting sexual abuse/harassment
discomfort, as part of misogyny discussion process 123–124
distancing technique 65
distraction (5Ds of Bystander Intervention) 92–93, 96, 97, 105
documentation (5Ds of Bystander Intervention) 93–94
domestic abuse 11, 134
dominance 25, 42, 43, 54, 55, 103, 107, 138, 148, 151, 160; as desire 53; emotional cost of 150
double standards in behaviour policies 157

drama, using, to tackle MVAWG 149–150
Dublin City University, Anti-Bullying Centre 56

early intervention 47–48
eHarmony 22–23
emotional bullying 137
emotional experiences, validation of 70
emotional intelligence 48, 71, 158
emotional labour 13, 119, 159
emotional safety of staff who challenge culture 159–160
emotional suppression 44, 104, 163
empathetic interventions 122–126
empathy 45, 48, 54, 58, 66, 70, 73, 122, 126, 129, 131; creating space for 144, 147; rehearsing 149–150
'enemies' of incels 37
English classes, using, to tackle MVAWG 147–148
entitlement 53, 54, 55, 56, 131, 132, 136, 138, 141, 144; 'aggrieved' 27
Everyone's Invited website 2–4, 58
explanation, allure of 28–29, 117
external agencies, working with 146

face-to-face harmful sexual behaviour 7
false rape reports 5, 44–45
fatherhood rights 43, 45
The Fathering project 43
female genital mutilation (FGM) 8, 135
femininity, and rape culture 5
'flashing' 8
forced marriage 135
friendship groups, warning signs in 141

'game' (seduction skills) 24
The Game (Strauss) 42
gender 132, 136; as relational, not adversarial 126
gender futures, shared positive vision of 126

169

Index

gender roles 103
Glamour magazine 80
Global Equality Collective 61
grooming 28

'hard man' persona 137–138
height, average, of incels 36–37
historical norms 103
History classes, using, to tackle MVAWG 149
honour-based abuse 135
hypergamy 21–22

I May Destroy You (TV series) 2
imaged-based harassment *see* sexual images
The Incel Rebellion (Sugiura) 17–18, 36
incel-related radicalisation 68–71; children at risk of 68; indicators of 68–69; strategies to counteract 69–71
incels (involuntary celibates) 19–20, 21, 23–38; average height 36–37; Chads, Stacies, and Beckies 24; connection, online and real-world 38; 'enemies' of 37; mental health 27–28, 34, 37; and politics 37; and racism 35; and violence 29–35, 37–38; who they are 36–38; why people become incels 27–29
Incels.me website 32–33
indecent exposure 8
influencers *see* toxic influencers
intervention: early 47–48; empathetic 122–126; *see also* 5Ds Model of Bystander Intervention
isolation 28
'It's Just Everywhere' report (UK Feminista) 9–10

Jaki, S. 32–33
jealousy 139, 140, 143, 148, 153
jokes: paedophile 99; sexual 5, 87, 97, 104, 111
Journal of Positive Behaviour Interventions 119

Kalish, R. 27
Keeping Children Safe in Education (DfE) 8–9, 81, 83–86, 87–88, 90, 154
Kimmel, M. 27
kindness 40, 43, 45, 48, 49, 66, 70, 71, 107, 133
Kraus, A. 54

language: to use and avoid 126–129, 143; *see also* scripted responses
listening 47, 142, 145, 147, 159
Livett, PJ, tips for talking to boys about sex and pornography 64–68
local organisations, building partnerships with 154–155
loneliness 23, 27, 28, 29, 37, 47, 55, 63, 68, 69, 116–117, 126
'love bombing' 57
Love Respect website 153

Malamuth, N. 53
male attractiveness, hierarchy of 25–26
Male Violence Against Women and Girls (MVAWG) 131–162; in the classroom 136–139; continuum of harm 135; culture of control 139; defining the problem 133; identification 144–145; prevention 143–144; school culture as enabler of 156–160; spectrum of 134–135; staff blind spots and risk of misinterpretation 141–142; warning signs 139–142; whole-school response to *see* whole-chool approach
manhood, and rape culture 77
manosphere 13, 17–50, 103; accessibility of disturbing content 18; black pill ideology 21, 28, 32; blue and red pill ideology 20–21; hierarchy of male attractiveness 25–26; hypergamy and 80:20 principle 21–22; incel community *see* incels; Men's Rights Activists (MRAs) 43–45; MGTOWs (Men Going Their Own Way) 39–40;

Index

naming the 45–7; Pick-Up Artists (PUAs) 24, 40–43; Prevent and 19–20; what schools and teachers can do about 45–48
masculinity/masculinities 144; offering alternative narratives of 71, 107; positive, modeling of 70; and rape culture 5
The Matrix (movie) 20
media studies, using, to tackle MVAWG 150
Men's Rights Activists (MRAs) 43–45
mental health 27–28, 34, 37, 45
mentorship 47, 71, 144
MGTOWs (Men Going Their Own Way) 39–40
misogyny 12, 13–14, 75; as armour 122; assemblies as starting point for student education on 102–105; avoiding tackling 120–121; as banter 117; as confusion 118; cost of not responding to 121–122; defining 102; empathetic interventions 122–126; language to use and avoid when talking about 126–129; as a mask 115–116; pitfall responses to avoid 119–121; as reaction to rejection 116–117; 'sliding scale' of misogynistic thinking 124–125; ten tips to discuss misogyny effectively with boys 122–126; whole-school approach to tackling *see* whole-school approach
modeling: positive masculinity 70; vulnerability 47; *see also* role models
moral lectures 120
MVAWG *see* Male Violence Against Women and Girls

name-calling, sexualised 5, 6, 7, 110, 134
National Audit Office (NAO) 134
National Education Union (NEU) 9
National Police Chief's Council (NPCC) 11, 132

negging 42
non-contact forms of harmful sexual behaviour 7
'Normies' 24
NSPCC, *Talk PANTS* 153

Office for National Statistics (ONS) 134
Ofsted 4, 5–7, 134
OKCupid 23
omega males 25
online harmful sexual behaviour 6, 7, 11, 88, 104, 134–135; *see also* pornography; sexual images, sending and circulating of
online mimicry, watching out for 71
OnlyFans models 112
Oxford University 22–23

paedophile jokes 99
parent resource bank 72
parental responsibility 165
parents, engaging and supporting 71–73, 107, 109–110, 152–155
partnerships with local organisations 154–155
pastoral teams, working with 71, 158
patriarchy 120, 149
PE, using, to tackle MVAWG 151
peacocking 42
peer dynamics 103, 109, 132, 141, 143, 164
peer education 144
'performance' myth, debunking the 65
Phillipson, B. 80
photographs *see* sexual images
Pick-Up Artists (PUAs) 24, 40–43
police involvement 93
Police School Liaison Officers 155
policy documents: barriers to producing 89–91; schools' production of own 83, 85; statutory *see* Keeping Children Safe in Education (DfE)
politics, and incel ideology 37
politics classes, using, to tackle MVAWG 150

171

Index

Ponsford, N. 61–63
Pornhub 52–53
pornography 112; addiction 66–67; impact on attitudes 51–55; talking to boys about 63–68; violence in 52–53
positive masculinity, modeling of 70
poster campaigns 107, 110, 113
power/power dynamics 103, 131, 132, 135, 136, 144, 149–150
prevalence of sexual harassment 6–7
Prevent 19–20
Prevent referrals 19
prevention of MVAWG: involving boys without alienating them 143–144; whole-school culture 143
primary schools 58–60
promiscuity 5, 76, 78
PSHE (Personal, Social, Health and Economic Education) 148
psychological factors 103
PTSD 27, 34
public tellings-of 119–120

racism, incels and 35
radicalisation *see* incel-related radicalisation
rape 7, 85, 86, 134; boys/men as victims of 5, 78–79; decriminalisation of 5
Rape Crisis England and Wales (RCEW) 4–5, 8
Rape Crisis South London 77
rape culture 1, 2, 4–5, 9, 76–79
rape reports: charges resulting from 5, 134; false 5, 44–45
Rape and Sexual Abuse Support Centre 77
red and blue pill ideology 20–21
Reddit 32; r/MensRights thread 44
Refuge 153
rejection 27; misogyny as reaction to 116–117
reporting sexual abuse/harassment 6, 9–10, 138, 144–145; anonymous 108, 110; *see also* rape reports

responding to MVAGW/sexual harassment *see* sexual harassment, how to respond to; whole-school approach
responsibility 107, 131, 136; of adults 164; of boys 166; giving boys roles of 71; of parents 165; of schools 164–165; shared, parent–school 72–73, 107, 109–110
restorative justice 146
Review of Sexual Abuse in Schools and Colleges (Ofsted) 4, 5–7
ricecel 35
Right to Be 92, 93
Rodger, E. 29–31, 33
role models 158–159; positive 47, 48, 66, 107, 110
romance, control framed as 136–137
Romeo and Juliet 98–99
RSE (Relationships and Sex Education) 148–149
rumours, spreading of sexist 111, 134

safe spaces, creation of 70
safeguarding guidance/procedures: gaps and inconsistencies 10, 157–158; schools' own 83, 85, 157–158; statutory 8–9, 81, 83–86, 87–88, 90, 154
school culture *see* whole-school culture
science classes, using, to tackle MVAWG 151
scripted responses 98–101, 107, 109, 110–113
self-worth 27
SEN teams, working with 71
Serious Crime Act (2015) 134
Setty, E. 123, 124, 126
sex: normalisation of curiosity about 65; talking to boys about 63–68
sexual assault 7, 134; definition of 8, 86; trivialisation of 5, 76, 77
sexual comments 87, 97, 104, 111
sexual experiences: discussing 113; pressure to have had 76, 78

Index

sexual harassment 1–4, 8–9, 75–114, 134; behaviours 82–83, 87–89, 104; child-on-adult 10, 79–82; definition of 8; documentation 93–95; prevalence of 6–7, 9; reporting of 6, 9–10; school policy documents, barriers to 89–91; school policy documents, lack of 10; school policy documents, production of 83, 85; statistics 9, 104; statutory safeguarding guidance 8–9, 81, 83–86, 87–88, 90; toleration of 76, 77; video recording of 94

sexual harassment, how to respond to: 5Ds Model of Bystander Intervention 92–97, 105; *Come Off It* method 97–98, 105; scripted responses 98–101, 107, 109, 110–113

sexual images: sending and circulating of 5, 6, 78, 88, 104, 111; *see also* pornography

sexual jokes 5, 87, 97, 104, 111

Sexual Market Value (SMV) 21–22, 24

Sexual Offences Act (2003) 85

sexual rumours, spreading of 111, 134

sexual violence 7–8, 76, 85–87, 134

sexualised name-calling 5, 6, 7, 110, 134

shame/shaming 9, 47, 62, 65, 144, 148, 153, 165

shared responsibility, school–parent 72–73, 107, 109–110

sigma males 26

silence: culture of 141; girls' 138–139

'sliding scale' of misogynistic thinking 124–125

social media 7, 55–57; algorithms 55–56, 61; *see also* Reddit; TikTok; Tinder; YouTube

social networks, absence of real-world 28

social ostracism 6

social rejection *see* rejection

socialisation 103

sociology classes, using, to tackle MVAWG 150

Soma Sara 2–4

Speckhard, A. 33–34

'Stacies' 24

staff blind spots 141–142, 156

staff training 10, 106–107, 109

staffroom culture 156–157

statistics: domestic abuse 134; false rape reports 5; sexual harassment 9, 104

Strauss, N. 42

student-created anti-misogyny slogans 107–108, 110

Sugiura, L. 17–18, 36

suicidal thoughts 27, 34, 37

support workers, sexual harassment of 10

talking about sex and pornography with boys, tips for 64–68

Tate, A. 55, 57, 58, 150

teacher bias 1–2, 156

teachers: blindspots 141–142, 156; staffroom culture 156–157; training 10, 106–107, 109; unawareness of any sexism policies 10; underestimation of the problem 6; women, sexual harassment of 79–82

tech-enabled VAWG 11

'That's inappropriate', overuse of 120

TikTok 56–57

Tinder 22, 23

Tinder Experiments II (blog) 22

Tokunaga, R. S. 54

tone of a school 156

tone of voice 126, 129

touching, unwanted 7, 8, 9, 111

toxic influencers 51, 55–58, 103, 150; impact on attitudes 57–58

trauma-informed practice 145–146

trivialisation of sexual assault 5, 76, 77

173

Index

UK Feminista 9–10, 77, 120
uncertainty, as part of misogyny discussion process 123
Unison 10
unwanted touching 7, 8, 9, 111
upskirting 88, 104

values, talking about 66, 125
victim blaming 4, 76, 77
video recording of harassment 94
videos *see* sexual images
violence: against other boys as red flag 138; incels and 29–35, 37–38; in pornography 52–3
Violence Against Women and Girls (VAWG) 10–11, 14; *see also* Male Violence Against Women and Girls (MVAWG)
vulnerability 71; modeling 47; as strength 49, 70

warning signs of MVAWG 139–142; boys showing concerning patterns 140–141; girls at risk 139–140; in peer dynamics and friendship groups 141
'We're better than that' slogan 107–108, 110
Whittaker, J. 27, 29, 36
whole-school approach 11, 101–102, 106–110; culture 146–147; curriculum 147–151; disciplinary action and restorative approaches 146; trauma-informed practice 145–146; working with external agencies 146; working with parents and wider community 152–155
whole-school culture 143, 145, 146–147, 165; double standards in behaviour policies 157; emotional safety for staff who challenge the culture 159–160; role models and representation 158–159; safeguarding gaps and inconsistent follow-through 157–158; and staffroom attitudes 156–157; as unwitting enabler of misogyny 156–160
Women and Equalities Committee 81–82
women teachers, sexual harassment of 79–82
womenhood, and rape culture 77
Women's Aid 57, 153
Worker Protection (Amendment of Equality Act 2010) Act (2023) 80–81
Wright, P. J. 54

Xvideos 52–53

YouGov 58
YouTube 56–57

For Product Safety Concerns and Information please contact our EU representative GPSR@taylorandfrancis.com
Taylor & Francis Verlag GmbH, Kaufingerstraße 24, 80331 München, Germany

www.ingramcontent.com/pod-product-compliance
Lightning Source LLC
Chambersburg PA
CBHW050905160426
43194CB00011B/2297